VISIONARIES INTERVIEWS WITH FASHION DESIGNERS

VISIONARIES
INTERVIEWS
WITH
FASHION
DESIGNERS

SUSANNAH FRANKEL

V&A Publications

First published by V&A Publications, 2001
V&A Publications,
160 Brompton Road
London SW3 1HW
© Susannah Frankel 2001
Interviews originally published in The
Independent © The Independent
All interviews taken from The Guardian
© Guardian Newspapers Ltd

Susannah Frankel asserts her moral right
to be identified as the author of this book

Designed by Daren Ellis

Jacket: Photography: Robert Wyatt. Styling:
Lucy Ewing. Hair and make-up: Liz Daxauer.
Model: Rebecca Brenan @ Take Two. Hand-
painted ballgown: Valentino haute couture,
spring/summer 1998.

Frontispiece: Photography: Jane McLeish.
Styling: Rebecca Leary. All clothes Comme
des Garçons, spring/summer 1997.

ISBN 1 85177 364 9

A catalogue record for this book is
available from the British Library

Origination: Colorlito, Milan
Printed in Italy by
Artegrafica

V&A Publications
160 Brompton Road
London SW3 1HW
www.vam.ac.uk

For Jim and Joseph

My grateful thanks to the following:

Alan Rusbridger, editor of *The Guardian*, Simon Kelner, editor of *The Independent*, and Jefferson Hack, editor of *Dazed & Confused*, for permission to use the interviews in this book.

Deborah Orr, my formidable editor at *Weekend Guardian*, and Mark Porter, art director at *Weekend Guardian*, who were an inspiration to work with.

Susannah Barron and Romaine Lillie for their patience assisting me at *The Guardian*, and my current team at *The Independent*: Beth Dadswell for organising a very hectic department, Rebecca Lowthorpe for her tireless efforts, and Sophia Neophitou with whom it is a privilege to work.

Andrew Tuck, editor of *The Independent on Sunday Review*, and Lisa Markwell, editor of *The Independent* magazine, for their friendship and support.

Sally Brampton, Iain R. Webb and Paula Reed for their generosity and knowledge and for helping me out of many a sticky situation. Colin McDowell for his *bons mots*.

The photographers and stylists who worked so hard and with such creativity on the pictures in this book, on a shoe-string budget, in particular Lucy Ewing, Robert Wyatt and Jane McLeish. Thanks too to all the photographers and stylists I have worked with who haven't been included.

The models, hair and make-up artists who appear in this book – there isn't room to credit them all.

Claire Wilcox, curator of 20th-century dress at the Victoria & Albert Museum, for suggesting the publication of the book in the first place and for coming up with a title. Mary Butler, head of publications at V&A Enterprises, for agreeing to go ahead. And Rachel Connolly, for her keen eye and patience with the editing process.

Daren Ellis, the art director of this book.

Tanya Sarne, Alex Barlow and the staff at Ghost for many an uproarious fashion moment and for my wedding dress. Janet Fischgrund, Amie Witton, Sidonie Barton and all at Alexander McQueen for being the best fashion friends.

Jo-Ann Furniss for keeping me company on the 'phone.

Lucy, for listening.

Lastly, a very special thanks to my mother and father for introducing me to their colourful world and for their constant love and support.

Over the last decade Susannah Frankel's contribution to the world of fashion journalism has been essential reading for anyone interested in fashion, and has converted many who were not. The V&A is grateful to *The Guardian*, *The Independent* and *Dazed & Confused* for the opportunity to publish these remarkable interviews in a more permanent form. Their reissue at this time complements the V&A's Radical Fashion exhibition, which many of the designers are taking part in.

Accompanied by specially commissioned photographs, these unique portraits were intended to capture significant moments in each designer's career, in some cases before they reached the heights of fame. As a collection, they reflect the development of the world's most innovative fashion in the late 20th and early 21st century. It is to Susannah Frankel's credit that she has made conceptual fashion accessible to a suspicious press and public. In the process she has become a fearless champion of its cause.

Although an impassioned writer, Frankel is ultimately a realist; she believes fashion, for all its artistry, is a high craft rather than an art. Her articles are notable for their insight and honesty but they are also entertaining. They provide a glimpse into the motivation and lives of some of the most enigmatic creative spirits in contemporary fashion, while also documenting the cultural climate of the day. Through them, the common reader shares Frankel's sense of privilege, for she asks all the questions we would like to, if we had the chance.

Claire Wilcox
Curator for 20th-Century Dress, Victoria & Albert Museum

In December 1995 Alan Rusbridger, editor of *The Guardian*, tracked me down – I was having my teeth cleaned, glamorously enough – to inform me that I had been given the job of fashion editor of *The Guardian*. A decidedly reserved character, suffice it to say that he seemed rather taken aback by the fact that, in my excitement, I could barely find the voice to respond. Never have I been so elated, so proud – and so completely terrified. In honour of my new post, I rushed out and bought several hundred pounds' worth of books – I needed a fashion history lesson, I thought, fast – and proceeded to drive my nearest and dearest half mad with my anxiety and excitement, my almost constant (fashion) questions.

Fast forward two months and I found myself, almost paralysed by fear, sitting next to Sally Brampton, my fashion mentor, in the front row of John Galliano's debut collection for the house of Givenchy, held in a vast sports stadium in the suburbs of Paris. All the legendary commentators were there: Anna Wintour of American *Vogue*, Suzy Menkes of the *International Herald Tribune*, Amy Spindler and Holly Brubach of the *New York Times*. And then there was me. As one outfit after another came out, worn by the world's most beautiful women – a sinuous black *Le Smoking*, a bias-cut silk fringed slip in dusty rose, an over-blown ballgown with rustling skirts – my fear quickly subsided. I was, I realised, as the hairs stood up on the back of my neck and the tears sprang to my eyes, quite the luckiest woman in the world.

Several years – and many hundreds and even thousands of fashion shows later – I still feel that way. It says quite something for the great names in fashion that they continue to move me, season after season, with their proposals of how women might like to dress.

Of course, there have been less than salubrious moments. Pity me standing in central Paris in the pouring rain with my mobile phone, filing news live from a show, suddenly entirely lost for words. My friend Iain R. Webb sprang to the rescue, as he has many times since, dictated the story to me and, hey presto, there it was, ghost written, in the paper the next day. And there was the time I filed a 500-word review in praise of Yohji Yamamoto – a personal favourite – to copy, only to find the following morning that his name had been miraculously transformed into Wohji Yamamoto in the auspicious pages of *The Guardian*. Quite how the copy taker in question could have interpreted 'Y for yellow' for, well, 'W for wally', frankly, remains a mystery. Thankfully, Wohji, ever the perfect gentleman, didn't seem too concerned. Neither did the famous 'Australian' designer, Helmut Lang, 'Georgio' Armani, or American first lady of fashion, Donna 'Karam', for that matter.

Alexander McQueen once told me that being interviewed by me was like being on the psychiatrist's couch. I'm not quite sure whether to take this as a compliment or not. I do know, however, that all the characters profiled in this book have been exceedingly generous with their time and patient with my prying. I feel privileged to have met them all.

I hope that the dates printed at the start of each piece make it clear that time has passed since they were written. Gucci, for example, has since become one of the world's most powerful fashion empires, and Tom Ford is now also at the creative helm of Yves Saint Laurent. Issey Miyake has since given up his signature collection to concentrate solely on A-POC: clothing cut from a single, very lovely tube of cloth. Zandra Rhodes is further down the line with her museum of fashion and textiles in Bermondsey, although it has not officially opened as yet. Alexander McQueen no longer designs for Givenchy but has Gucci as a backer instead, and is probably the most famous designer in the world.

Each interview was carried out at a pivotal time in the career of the designer concerned: anything from a major anniversary or a particularly challenging collection to a welcome revival or global expansion inspired me. I hope that the finished pieces, accompanied by the original images that were commissioned to run alongside, capture important moments in time and, without wishing to appear overly grand, preserve them more permanently in fashion history.

I could never have foreseen a career in fashion journalism – I studied English at Goldsmiths' in London where I was born and bred. Having said that, my parents probably planted the seed. Thanks to them – my joyful mother and my immaculate, gentle father – I grew up in the heart of the Sixties youthquake, in the sartorially explosive environs of the then supremely fashionable King's Road. Not many little girls were lucky enough to meet Manolo Blahnik at the age of seven. I have my mother's best friend, Amanda, who I still love dearly, to thank especially for that. I still remember vividly the exotic fragrance of Jungle Gardenia that always surrounded her, her tousled mass of blonde hair, her extraordinary Antony Price dresses, her glittering, jangling jewellery and her glamour-filled handbags. The only thing that excited me more than watching my mother getting dressed to go out – sticking the heels of her shoes to her narrow feet with double-sided sticky-tape, applying lipstick a shade paler than her mouth and scattering sparkle here, there and everywhere – was seeing Amanda in action. A little girl couldn't wish for a more beautiful source of inspiration.

If fashion can be in your blood, I suppose it must have been in mine, because to say that I took to the subject like a duck to water would be something of an understatement. I love fashion: for its life-enhancing beauty, for its constantly exciting and unpredictable nature and, most of all, for its celebration of the female form. As for the designers themselves – who could wish for more brilliant subjects? Talented, extraordinary and, above all and almost without exception, extremely funny, they continue to amaze me. I hope they always will.

01
ALEXANDER MCQUEEN

SO WHERE DO YOU THINK YOUR GENIUS COMES FROM?

IS THAT SUPPOSED TO BE A SERIOUS QUESTION?

Portrait: Anne Deniau

Alexander McQueen
The Independent fashion magazine, autumn/winter 2000
Fashion photography: Mert Alas and Marcus Piggott
Backstage photography: Anne Deniau
All clothes Alexander McQueen, autumn/winter 2000

The first time I visited Alexander McQueen at his Islington home, he took me by the hand and led me upstairs, announcing: 'Come on. I want to show you my arsehole.'

It says much for the sheer charm of fashion's favourite wunderkind that, though fairly appalled at the prospect, I nonetheless followed him up the stairs and into his bedroom, only to discover that the treat in store was not – thankfully – what it seemed, but an enormous oil painting, facing his unmade bed and dominating the entire room. With its shadowy black centre, surrounded by a mottled starburst of colour, the painting is, in fact, exaggerated in its proportions to the point of abstraction, but after an introduction such as this one it left little to the imagination.

Although trying to maintain my composure, I couldn't help but react, squeaking with nervous laughter (as much out of relief as anything else), while McQueen, beaming happily from ear to ear, looked proudly on.

'Do you like it?' he enthused, as if this were some sort of delight he had prepared for me especially.

Then, hooting with glee (or was it derision?), he turned on his heel and ran back downstairs, leaving me standing there, not knowing where to look, both embarrassed and even faintly disapproving, and with the distinct impression that I had, in fact, simply been on the receiving end of a ritual meted out to all his friends and family. (Pity his poor nan.)

There are those who might say, of course, that this is quintessential Alexander McQueen. He is, after all, the so-called 'bad boy of British fashion', a designer who has made something of a career out of shocking not only the press and public but also the supposedly shock-proof fashion industry he works within. (Even in fashion's inner circle, the rumour holds that the glorious orifice hanging up on his bedroom wall is his own.)

This is typical behaviour then, not only of the tabloid incarnation of the designer but of the man who has gone on to become the stuff of fashion legend. Alexander McQueen: working-class oik/skinhead/gay raver, the 'yob amongst snobs', a man who has run riot through the precious artistry of fashion, in his battered trainers and jeans, everywhere from London's fashionable East End to the monied Givenchy atelier in Paris.

As an apprentice tailor on Savile Row, McQueen famously inscribed the words 'I am a cunt' in the lining of a jacket destined for the Prince of Wales. Later, as a designer in his own right, he pioneered the bumster, trousers with a waistband so low that anyone brave enough to wear them would parade their buttocks for all to see.

From the outside, it seemed, McQueen deliberately turned

any controversy that might spring up in his wake to his advantage. His collections had wildly provocative titles: Highland Rape, The Golden Shower. (The latter was later renamed simply 'Untitled' because American Express, McQueen's long-time sponsor, objected to its sexually explicit connotations.) His sets came complete with everything from smashed up cars, their bonnets spewing acrid smoke, to caged ravens. McQueen's models, meanwhile, were subjected variously to having their heads encased in a cloud of white net swarming with live butterflies, to standing in circles that rotated before duly bursting into flames.

As if all that weren't enough, the designer has also always been the master of the soundbite, happily bad-mouthing establishment designers and displaying an arrogance that ensured he made the headlines each and every time he opened his mouth. 'I don't give a shit what other French designers think of me, I'll bring French chic to Paris', he once said, and this when the whole of that capital was up in arms at his appointment at Givenchy.

Still aged only 30, McQueen's extraordinary imagination and power to provoke at the drop of a hat has meant that he has become the best-known, most talked about fashion designer in the world. But although it is true that, initially, he revelled in the adulation and was not immediately averse to the glamour that went with it, exploits such as these are not without their drawbacks.

Give the press an image, after all, and they will be more than happy first to run with it, then hammer it home. Pretty soon it will become all they see, no matter how ambitious your ideas or how brilliantly you express them.

To the press McQueen is a godsend – the temptation to reduce him to any number of stereotypes has proved simply too great to resist. He's the 'working-class lad from a family of taxi-drivers', the cheeky chappy always to be relied on where calling a spade a shovel is concerned, the aloof, arrogant essence of Cool Britannia, surrounded by his equally fashionable (and impenetrable) circle of friends. These and more have become easy ways to patronise the designer and thereby avoid any serious consideration of his work. Alexander McQueen has travelled the route from 'enfant terrible' to bona fide 'genius' in only five years, with very little in between. Suffice to say, this was the only way the press could deal with him.

And if this seems an awfully long way to have come, it is worth noting that both monikers are equally clichéd, and ultimately throwaway. The fact that interviewers have consistently fixated on McQueen's East End accent, his

constant use of expletives and vulgar ribald humour, has all too often reduced McQueen into just another example of that hoary old chestnut, the noble savage. More than one profile has even gone so far as to refer to his 'adenoidal snuffling' and the fact that, at the Givenchy atelier, he communicates via charade-like hand movements to make himself understood. For his part, McQueen has never made any bones about the fact that – like most other Englishmen – he simply doesn't speak French.

But lurking somewhere beneath it all is the man born Lee Alexander McQueen – the same as he ever was: as gentle, complicated, sensitive and charming as he can indeed be brutish, childish, arrogant and rude. Most importantly, this is a man who has demonstrated the determination to finally achieve the ambition he has nurtured ever since he was a small child.

With McQueen then, it is safe to say, nothing is quite as it seems.

Lee Alexander McQueen grew up in East London, the youngest of six children (two brothers, three sisters). He uses his middle rather than his first name when he works because he was signing on when he started out and 'didn't want to walk into the dole office one day and be recognised because I'd been in *The Sunday Times*'. His father is a cab driver, his mother a genealogist who went to work, teaching social history, only after her youngest son turned 16. Typically, her occupation is not often referred to.

McQueen shares with his mother a passionate interest in his heritage: he continues to include the McQueen tartan in current collections and, lest anyone think otherwise, the aforementioned Highland Rape collection was, in fact, intended as a comment on the rape of the Highlands at the hands of the British, not an assault on the world's most fêted models by its most fêted designer.

'Scotland for me is a harsh and cold and bitter place,' McQueen says today. 'It was even worse when my great, great grandfather used to live there. I have no respect for what the English did there, they wiped whole families out. The reason I'm patriotic about Scotland is because I think it's been dealt a really hard hand. It's marketed the world over as, you know, fucking haggis, fucking tartan, fucking bagpipes. But no one ever puts anything back into it. I hate it when people romanticise Scotland. There's nothing romantic about its history. What the British did there was nothing short of genocide.'

Neither, for the record, says McQueen, did he ever smear models' thighs with blood or attach tampons to the fronts of their skirts for this collection. It says much for the stature of the designer, however, that this has become the stuff of urban mythology. 'I never did that – never,' he says. However violent his imagery, it is safe to say that this is rather more crude than anything he would come up with.

McQueen went to school at Rokeby, the local all-boys comprehensive where, he says, he spent most of his time drawing clothes. 'I was literally three years old when I started drawing. I did it all my life, through primary school, secondary school, all my life. I always, always wanted to be a designer. I read books on fashion from the age of twelve. I followed designers' careers. I knew Giorgio Armani was a window-dresser, Emanuel Ungaro was a tailor.'

Given the brute maleness of his environment, he must, presumably, have been subject to quite some flak.

'No. People just ignored me. That was fine. I was doing it for myself. But I always knew I would be something in fashion. I didn't know how big, but I always knew I'd be something.'

After school, the young McQueen passed the time bird-watching from the roof of the tower block where he lived. He was a member of the Young Ornithologists Society of Great Britain. 'It's almost like Kez, isn't it?' he says. 'I'm sure my story's no different to a lot of people from East London.'

He left school, aged 16, with one O level and one A level, both in art, which, ironically, was not enough to earn him a place on a foundation course. 'I would never have got into Saint Martins,' he says. To earn pocket money, he started working as a pot-boy in the local watering hole. But not for long. In 1986 his mother saw a report on television on how Savile Row was lacking apprentices and was threatened with collapse.

'I went straight down there. I hardly had any qualifications when I left school. So I thought the best way to do it was to learn how to make the stuff, learn the construction of clothes properly and go from there.'

The first people he saw were Anderson & Sheppard who employed him on the spot. He worked there for two years before moving on to Gieves & Hawkes. 'I did trousers at Anderson & Sheppard and jackets at Gieves & Hawkes.' To this day, McQueen's tailoring is second to none. Unlike the majority of designers, he learned this particular aspect of his trade in the traditional manner and, however extreme his designs may be, they are nonetheless executed with all the precision of bespoke menswear.

From Savile Row, McQueen moved on to Bermans & Nathans, theatrical costumiers, cutting clothes for major London shows including *Les Miserables*. ('The work was great, but I couldn't stand the queens there, they drove me nuts.') There followed a brief stint working for Koji Tatsuno.

'His work was based on British tailoring with a mix of avant garde and I thought, there's nothing like this in London.'

When Tatsuno went bankrupt, a casualty of the late Eighties along with so many others, McQueen took the opportunity to move on to sunnier climes. One of the designer's more endearing characteristics is that, like a small and seriously motivated child, he remains unafraid to ask for what he wants, unlike most of us who are simply too uptight and, more importantly, too afraid of rejection to do so. If McQueen thought, even for a second, that his ambition was in danger of being thwarted, he didn't hesitate to approach someone, no matter how lofty, and simply ask for a job.

'There was nothing going on in London,' he says, 'and the biggest thing at that time was Romeo Gigli, he was everywhere. I thought this is the only person I want to work for. My sister was a travel agent. I got a flight, a one-way ticket to Milan. I was twenty years old. I walked into Romeo Gigli with the worst portfolio you've ever seen, full of costume design. They said they had nothing and they'd call me if anything came up. Anyway, I was walking down the street afterwards and this girl came up to me, screaming at me like a madwoman: "Stop, stop. Romeo wants to see you. He wants to see you tomorrow. Come back." I was hired.'

It was while working with Gigli that McQueen learned the power of the press.

'Gigli had all this attention,' he says, 'and I wanted to know why. It had very little to do with the clothes and more to do with him as a person. And that's fundamentally true of anybody. Any interest in the clothes is secondary to interest in a designer. You need to know that you're a good designer as well, though. You can't give that sort of bullshit without having a back-up. If you can't design, what's the point of generating all that hype in the first place?'

Just under a year later, McQueen found himself back in London. Gigli had split with his partner Carla Sozzani and the publicity machine that previously showered Italy's favourite designer with unabashed hyperbole had gone sour. 'I was on holiday when I heard about it,' McQueen says matter of factly. 'I never went back, never said goodbye, nothing.'

Instead, this pushed him to finally enter the hallowed portals of Central Saint Martins, where rather than attempting to enrol on a course, he applied for a teaching position.

'He came in for a job teaching pattern cutting,' Bobbie Hillson, founder-director of the by-now legendary Central Saint Martins postgraduate fashion course and teacher of, among others, John Galliano and Rifat Ozbek, has said. 'We didn't have one. I thought he was very interesting, and he clearly had terrific talent.' More impressive even than this though was McQueen's drive. 'To have left school at sixteen, studied at Savile Row, gone to Italy alone and found a job with Gigli – that was incredible. He was also technically brilliant, even though he'd never actually studied design. And still only twenty-one or twenty-two.'

'I don't think you can become a good designer, or a great designer, or whatever,' says McQueen. 'To me, you just are one. I think to know about colour, proportion, shape, cut, balance is part of a gene. My sister is an amazing artist. My brother is an amazing artist, amazing, much better than I am. The difference is, they thought they had no chance but to do a manual job. That's what really upsets me.'

Not so McQueen. He says that his time at Central Saint Martins was far from idyllic. He was used to earning his own money, then suddenly found himself living at home, squabbling with his parents, and his father in particular, who failed to understand his son's vocation. His aunt, Renie Holland, supported him at the time.

Professionally, from here on in, McQueen never looked back. His entire degree collection – spiky tailoring and even more spiky ideas – was bought by Isabella Blow, then fashion editor at *Vogue*, now fashion director of *The Sunday Times*, and a woman who knows a good thing when she sees one. As patron, muse and unofficial PR, Blow set about promoting McQueen as London's Next Big Thing. The heady combination of her considerable connections and his talent and energy was quite a force to be reckoned with. McQueen was by now well on his way. It is not insignificant that, despite the fickle nature of the world in which they both work, the two remain great friends to this day.

Looking back at McQueen's formative years as a designer, it is all too easy to see him as some sort of working class cliché, a shock merchant over and above anything else. To do so, however, would be to seriously under-estimate both his complexity and the scale of his ambition.

'Yeah, there has been this big thing about the East End yob made good,' he says, clearly irritated by the fact that he is having to address it once again. 'But, you know, the press started that, not me. The press started that, and I played on it. It's the Michael Caine syndrome, Pygmalion. It's not true. At the end of the day, you're a good designer

or not and it doesn't matter where you come from. But the press always wanted more. The East End boy who worked on Savile Row. The East End boy who worked wherever . . . Whatever . . . Everyone knows the story and it's tiring.'

McQueen's childhood was not an easy one. While he might object to being pigeon-holed, he is also the first to admit that he's got to where he has done despite considerable adversity.

On more than one occasion, Alexander McQueen has alluded to violence in his background, both directed towards himself and to those close to him. When he was eight years old he witnessed one of his older sisters' husbands – who has since died of a heart attack – beating her to within an inch of her life. It is perhaps for this reason that you can hurl pretty much any insult at McQueen and he will bounce right back, but call him a misogynist and you get a glimpse of the anger and determination that drives him.

'I was this young boy and I saw this man with his hands round my sister's neck, I was just standing there with her two children beside me . . . Everything I've done since then was for the purpose of making women look stronger, not naïve. And so, when everyone started saying I was a misogynist, that really freaked me out. They didn't know me. They didn't know what I had seen in my life. That was the first part of fashion that I hated – people labelling me without knowing me. You know, they can say what they like but they don't know me from Adam. I am constantly trying to reflect the way women are treated. It's hard to interpret that in clothes or in a show but there's always an underlying, sinister side to their sexuality because of the way I have seen women treated in my life. Where I come from, a woman met a man, got shagged, had babies, moved to Dagenham, two up two down, made the dinner, went to bed. That was my image of women. And I didn't want that. I wanted to get that out of my head.'

Even this season, McQueen has been accused of promoting negative images of femininity in the liberal press.

At his most recent show for Givenchy, he was attacked for not using models at all but mannequins in glass and fibreglass instead. 'It was nothing to do with what I think of models,' he told me at the time. 'I just think the couture client can be intimidated by the image of clothes on a very young girl. I wanted to give them a blank page to work with.' For his signature collection, The Overlook, he came under the spotlight for painting white stripes across models' eyes, rendering them both anonymous and expressionless.

'We're not talking about models' personal feelings here,' he says. 'We're talking about mine. Models are there to showcase what I'm about, nothing else. It's nothing to do with misogyny. It's all about the way I'm feeling about my life.' And the usually ebullient McQueen is currently going through a surprisingly bleak time. 'For the past year, I've been very unhappy because I've fallen in love with someone and it's been very difficult, it hasn't been working, because of my workload and all the other shit that goes with my job. To have all that pressure on your shoulders, to be responsible for all those people, all these lives. And then my personal life was going down the pan. I was just very depressed, you know.'

The Overlook is the name of the hotel in the book and film *The Shining*. Once again, McQueen's audience entered into the spirit of things, threatened by the prospect of sinister

and unpleasant things to come. And once again, McQueen came up with something, though eerie, more lovely and overtly romantic than anyone could have expected. In this way, the designer continues to undermine any prejudice and/or preconception. When things turn out to be other than they seem, as they do time and time again, this perhaps says rather more about McQueen's audience than the designer himself.

It is by now the stuff of fashion history that, aged 27, McQueen found himself – and no one was more surprised by this than the designer himself – heading up the house of Givenchy, known for its restrained elegance: Audrey Hepburn was Hubert de Givenchy's most famous muse. Overnight, and having designed no more than eight of his own collections in total, McQueen was forced to design ten collections a year.

In retrospect, he says, 'maybe I was too young to take on Givenchy. But nobody in my position would have done any different. I had to accept it.'

Tolerance is not what fashion is famous for, however. Although designers are finding themselves in the spotlight increasingly early on in their careers and are therefore forced to grow up, to a greater or lesser extent, in public, they will not be forgiven for putting a foot wrong. McQueen's first collection for Givenchy, and his first ever haute couture collection, put together in only eight weeks, was almost universally panned.

'I was twenty-seven years old and I'd done more than most designers in the history of fashion,' he says. 'I look at that first collection and me and Katy [England – McQueen's long-time creative collaborator], especially Katy, we worked so hard. We were so brought down by that experience, emotionally and spiritually. It was a fucking nightmare.'

McQueen has since gone on to become accepted, albeit grudgingly, by the French fashion establishment. However, while his shows for Givenchy have demonstrated increasing confidence and a surprisingly astute nose for the commercial, it is with the Alexander McQueen label that he has really made his mark, changing the face of fashion.

For his spring/summer '99 collection, shown in February 1999, he transformed Aimee Mullins, the first ever catwalk model with both legs amputated from the knee down, into a superstar overnight. McQueen met Mullins on a shoot he art directed for *Dazed & Confused*, shot by big-name photographer Nick Knight and featuring only models with severe physical disabilities, dressed in clothes by designers as diverse as Comme des Garçons, Hussein Chalayan and, of course, McQueen himself.

When word got out within the industry that the pair were working on this project, they were accused not only of exploitation but also sensationalism, despite the fact that nobody had actually seen a single image. As it turned out, this couldn't have been further from the truth. The pictures that came out of this collaboration are perhaps the most challenging in years. McQueen, once again, was demonstrating a sympathy with the underdog while, more importantly, undermining society's expectations of what is and isn't beautiful. By going on to introduce Mullins to the catwalk, meanwhile, he was also putting his money where his mouth was. It was a noble gesture, and one far from sensational. Mullins was styled to look just like every other model: her legs were hand-carved following a design by McQueen himself. Far from the freak show that many

predicted, she was allowed to do her job along with the rest of them, passing barely unnoticed. McQueen recognised in Mullins a determination as great as his own; small wonder then that he was only too happy to help her to achieve her long-term goal.

While McQueen's profile is now higher than it ever has been, it is one of the ironies of the designer fashion industry that you see very few people actually wearing his clothes. In department stores, many of which have been loyal to the designer since he started out, buyers can only invest a certain amount in each particular designer, after all. This is set to change.

London – up-and-coming Conduit Street, to be precise – is about to become home to the first ever Alexander McQueen store. This could be his most significant attempt to pursue his own aesthetic yet, a step towards independence and permanence outside the constraints of the industry.

'Having money hasn't changed me,' says Alexander McQueen, as our meeting draws to a close. 'It's made my life worse, if anything. You get people coming up to you who you knew before you were famous that didn't come up to you before. I'm a clever designer. I can do what the client wants. But I'm prepared to forget about money if it affects my creativity because, remember, I started off with nothing. I started off on the dole. And I can do it again.

'I've never gone under, never been bankrupt and everything I do has a solid grounding, it's not on a whim. I suppose I'm the most successful designer in England because I knew how to market myself. It's always been part of my strategy to give people something they recognise, an attitude they can recognise. Some designers are so airy fairy, people can't connect with them, and that's where my working-class background can help, because people can relate to me, to a normal person who just happens to be a fashion designer.

'I'm someone who knows what the world is about. I have a point of view. Sometimes people might not like it but then it's not the designer's job to care about what people think. It's just his point of view. And it's a valid point of view. People can take me as they find me. Whatever else I've done, I've never tried to be something I'm not.'

I finally pluck up the courage to ask Alexander McQueen whether the celebrated painting on his bedroom wall is, in fact, a portrait.

'Well that's just typical,' he chides, this time attempting to play the outraged party himself. 'You know, when my little niece comes round she always says, "Mummy, Mummy, take me upstairs and show me that sunflower."

'Anyway,' he continues, clearly beginning to enjoy himself, 'it's far too clean to be mine.'

Just as I'm making to leave and thinking, perhaps, the painting has no significance beyond the fact that its owner likes the way it looks, McQueen finally stumbles upon its raison d'être, as if suddenly realising it for the first time himself.

'It's just like the fashion world that arsehole,' he blurts out with a childish enthusiasm and quite oblivious to any ramifications. 'Full of shit.'

Alexander McQueen's clear blue eyes, round like pebbles, are suddenly wide like the proverbial saucers. He seems to me to have never looked happier.

'I love that picture,' he says.

02 SONIA RYKIEL

DID YOU HAVE A STRONG SENSE OF YOUR PHYSICAL SELF AS A CHILD?

I WAS SO UGLY WHEN I WAS BORN – WITH MY HAIR SO RED. MY MOTHER SAID TO ME: 'YOU CAN DO EVERYTHING YOU WANT, BUT YOU HAVE TO BE INTELLIGENT'. BECAUSE I WASN'T PRETTY, I HAD TO BE FANTASTIC. AFTER THAT, I TURNED IT TO MY ADVANTAGE. I WAS SO STRONG. I DIDN'T CARE. I THOUGHT TO MYSELF: 'I'M A RED-HEADED GIRL AND I'M STRONG, SO DON'T TOUCH ME'.

Portrait: Sarah Moon

Sonia Rykiel
**A version of this article was published on 10 October 1998 in The Guardian Weekend magazine;
a later version appeared on 13 November 1999 in The Independent Saturday magazine.
Photography: Justin Smith. Styling: Sophia Neophitou
All clothes Sonia Rykiel, autumn/winter 1999**

Madame Sonia Rykiel is a renaissance woman. As well as having maintained her position as one of France's foremost fashion designers for more than 30 years, she is an acclaimed novelist (the titles of her books – *Je La Voudrais Etre Nue*; *Les Levres Rouges* – are worth the price of the volume alone), an artist (she has illustrated children's fairytales), and an interior designer (Rykiel has reworked the interior of two Paris hotels). In 1994 she even turned her hand to music, recording a duet with Malcolm McLaren: 'My name is Malcolm McLaren. And you?', asks McLaren. 'Sonia Rykiel,' whispers she in her cartoonish French tone.

If further proof were needed of her stature in French culture, Rykiel is also the proud recipient of the Officier de l'Ordre des Arts et Lettres and the Officier de l'Ordre National de l'Ordre de la Legion d'Honneur. Above all, however, fashion is her métier. With Yves Saint Laurent, she was responsible for dressing the bright young things that earned the Rive Gauche its élitist and bohemian name.

'Rykiel captured in her "poor-boy" sweaters – snuggled over braless bosoms above narrow, androgynous hips – the spirit of changing times,' Suzy Menkes of the *International Herald Tribune* has written. Certainly, her loosely formed but very sexy clothes were a far cry from the more formal and structured looks that came before them.

Today, aged 68 – an extraordinarily well-preserved 68 – Rykiel's creative powers show no sign of abating.

In 1997 the Queen of Knits sold no fewer than 90,000 of her signature sweaters. They came, as always, rainbow-striped, emblazoned with key words in diamanté, and, of course, in plain, existential black. Turnover that year was an impressive fr450 million.

I meet La Rykiel at her Paris flagship store on a corner of Boulevard St Germain, just a stone's throw from her favourite hang out, the Café Flore. The polished marble, black-and-white polka-dot carpet and black lacquer interior would be rather too chic to be true were it not for the sweetly naïve children's drawings on the stairwell. They were drawn by Rykiel's grandchildren, and her face lights up when she talks about them: 'I love my family. I love my sister [who designs accessories for the company]. I love my daughter, my son. I work with my sister all day long, and when I come home, I call her. And in the morning, I call her. I have another sister, who is a psychiatrist, and I call her twice a day. You know, even if we don't see each other sometimes, family, for me, is very, very important.'

The eldest of five daughters of a Russian Jewish family, Rykiel attributes her strength and intelligence, at least partly, to the fact that she was the least beautiful of her siblings. 'I had four sisters, and I was so ugly when I was born – with my hair so red – and my sisters were so beautiful. I was not jealous of my sisters, because I loved them absolutely violently, but my mother said to me, "You can do everything you want, but you have to be very intelligent." Because I wasn't pretty, I had to be fantastic. After that, I turned it to my advantage. I was so strong. I didn't care. I thought to myself, "I'm a red-headed girl and I'm strong, so don't touch me." '

Rykiel's appearance is, indeed, nothing short of fantastic: the deathly pallor of her face, so finely chiselled it seems almost skull-like, combined with the high drama of her clothes (for the most part, long, flowing and black), make for extraordinary viewing. She loves the artifice and dislikes what she describes as 'the natural look' in anyone else. 'I mean, you have to make the best of yourself,' she says, as if it were the most obvious thing in the world. 'Nobody is natural, only some exceptional people who are fantastic in the natural way. But I love the woman who has built her own personality into her appearance.'

Warhol was just one of many artists who have attempted to capture her for posterity. 'When I first saw my portrait by Andy Warhol, I was so upset. I couldn't understand how that was me. Now, I love it. You know, I meet a lot of painters and photographers who ask me to pose for them. I'm not proud of that. But I have the impression that I am a little bit *particulier*, individual – I have a particular figure.'

Rykiel came to design fashion purely by chance. 'I never decide nothing,' she says, decisively. 'It was not my purpose in life at all to be a fashion designer. I knew nothing about fashion. I was born in a very bourgeois, Jewish family. Nobody spoke about fashion, nobody spoke about clothing. It was forbidden completely. Then, I just married a man and my only ambition in life was to have ten children and to be like my mother – to make tea, to take care of the children, to go to a museum, to travel. But, unfortunately, I have only two children, and for me it was difficult to have any more.'

She soon set to working in her husband's clothing business, designing clothes that she herself liked to wear. Happily, other women liked them, too. After separating from her husband a few years later, Rykiel set up on her own.

'I knew nothing about fashion, and I didn't learn exactly the right way. You know, the couture designers know the way to cut and sew. I don't do it like that. It's just a reflection of me, of what I am. I am a woman, with children, with sisters. I know what young girls want. I'm not doing Russian one season, Chinese the next; I'm interested in fashion as a way of life.'

Little has really changed since that time. There are, of course, the subtle alterations that any great designer needs to make season after season to keep abreast of the new, but the Rykiel signature remains the same: long, skinny, black and very, very French.

'I have the impression that there are a lot of things I haven't done yet. An awful lot of things. I have the impression not of being young, but of being young in my work. Each day is a new day, and that's very lucky for me. And each day, when I awake, even if I have the impression that what I am doing is terrible, I begin again, and again.'

There are not many people who continue to express such drive and determination after 30 years at the top of their profession. This can only be a good thing: for Rykiel devotees and for French fashion. In a world where fashion relies increasingly on the spectacular and new, Rykiel has expressed her vision and stuck with it, as if her very existence depended on doing so. Long may she reign.

03
MARTIN MARGIELA

YOU SEEM UNINTERESTED IN FASHION AS A TREND-RELATED INDUSTRY – DO TRENDS AND THE REINVENTION OF THE WARDROBE SEASON AFTER SEASON BORE YOU?

NOT ALWAYS! WE DO NOT JUDGE OTHERS IN THEIR WORK, YET, FOR US, WE PREFER TO REFLECT THE REALITY OF OUR VIEW ON CLOTHES IN OUR COLLECTION. WE HAVE ALWAYS HAD GARMENTS THAT WE CONTINUE TO PROPOSE FOR MANY SEASONS IN A ROW (IN SOME INSTANCES TWELVE!). IT REMAINS MORE IMPORTANT FOR US THAT SOMEONE FINDS THEIR WAY OF DRESSING AS OPPOSED TO A WAY OF DRESSING AS PRESCRIBED BY ANYONE ELSE OR AN OVER-RIDING TREND.

Martin Margiela is the fashion designer's fashion designer. Cited by everyone from Rei Kawakubo of Comme des Garçons to Alexander McQueen as exceptionally innovative and inspired, in fashion circles he is universally respected – even revered.

The designer famously turns down requests for face-to-face interviews, preferring for questions to be faxed to his office and the answers faxed back with the following serving as introduction – or instruction, depending on which way you choose to look at it: 'We would like to point out that our answers to your questions have been reached as a team with the input of Mr Margiela and are offered here in the name of Maison Martin Margiela and not Martin Margiela as an individual. This explains the use of the first person plural instead of singular.'

If that weren't peculiar enough, it continues: 'We would prefer that all questions and answers be published in full.' Even in a famously dictatorial world, this is remarkably controlling, but then if anyone can get away with such behaviour, Martin Margiela can.

For those not entirely familiar with the murky workings of Martin Margiela's mind, consider, to begin with, the invitation to his autumn/winter '97 Paris show, something of a non-starter for the uninitiated. On finding, among a formidable pile of press material, a map of Paris emblazoned with the 'Printemps' logo and no trace of the designer's name in sight, one might have been forgiven for throwing it straight in the bin.

Back in London, the video of the aforementioned show – sent out afterwards to those unfortunate enough to have missed the point (and therefore also the show itself) – came dressed in its own little (Margiela-esque) white-linen sleeve. Suffice it to say that this only added to the confusion.

'Please turn your TV this way up,' said the white-on-black scrawl that flashed up in English, French and Japanese on the screen. 'Thank you.' The entire show was filmed on its side. Not only that, but Margiela's models, instead of merely strutting up and down a catwalk, had been delivered by double-decker bus to various different places in Paris where the fashion press had been advised to meet them. Dressed as they were in quite insane, if rather fetching fur wigs, and with shoulder-pads pinned to the outside of their clothes, it's small wonder that Parisian passers-by, also filmed on their sides for the purpose of the video and going about their daily work, couldn't help but stop and gawp at the spectacle in disbelief. Oom-pah-pah, oom-pah-pah went the accompanying live Belgian brass band.

Such cunning trickery is, of course, in no way out of character on the part of the designer. Margiela is famous, after all, for taking normal fashion-show requirements – minor details such as there being a catwalk, for example – and turning them on their heads. True to form then, on this particular occasion the obscurity of the invitation paled into insignificance in light of the show itself. On other occasions Margiela has shown his collections in the dark, with only fairy-lit umbrellas, carried by fashion assistants in white coats and following the models, to illuminate the clothes. Or he has simply decided not to show at all.

Are these just jokes? Is Margiela the Orson Welles of fashion? Couture's arch prankster? Is he, more loftily, the Thomas Pynchon of fashion? Or does Martin Margiela even actually exist? Is he simply a marketing tool, a figment of a particularly inspired press officer's all-too-fervent imagination?

These – apparently – are the facts.

He was born in Limbourg, Belgium, in 1959. At the age of 18 he went to Antwerp and studied fashion at the Academie Royale des Beaux Arts, then spent three years assisting Jean Paul Gaultier. He was said, at that time, to be in possession of fashionably large sideburns, although no pictorial evidence can be found to substantiate this claim.

In 1988 Margiela set up his own label in Brussels and burst onto the Paris fashion scene soon after, alongside Ann Demeulemeester and Helmut Lang. All three designers took the establishment by storm. This was not entirely surprising given that this was the decade that exemplified all that was brash and oozing with status, and Margiela in particular thought nothing of transforming a butcher's apron into an elegant dress, say, or a vintage tulle ballgown into a collection of jackets – all to very lovely effect.

Struggling to get to grips with his style, critics labelled it 'deconstruction': seams are reversed, loose threads hang down like cobwebs and tights are worn laddered – oh, and over shoes. Then there is the Margiela label. It's a blank square tacked roughly on to his clothes. Leave it where it is and it makes a mess of your jacket. Remove it and no one will even know your clothes are designer. And what's the point of that?

The idiosyncrasies of Margiela seem all the more peculiar given his appointment, announced in 1998, to Hermès, one of the world's most famous status labels. So far, this has been a very happy teaming – perhaps the most inspired, if, on the face of it, unlikely collaboration of them all.

Margiela's spring/summer '99 collection was a retrospective of his work of the past ten years, shown on 'real' people as opposed to just models and in the not-as-strange-as-they-might-be surroundings of a large and rather beautiful Paris town house. Perhaps the rather conservative proceedings (for Margiela) were due to the fact that, as the 20th collection shown to date, this could be seen as something of an anniversary, although this most elusive designer would probably rather die than describe it in such a mundane way. After all, that might entail some sort of celebration. And that would be far too frivolous. Instead, these images celebrate his great contribution to 20th-century fashion for him.

SF: Why did you choose to show your collection on people who aren't professional models?
MM: We have always chosen to present the collection on women varying in age and background. Our approach to the casting of our shows is the same as our views on

personality-based interviews, personal photo portraits of the designer, etc., etc. We have nothing against professional or 'top models' as individuals at all, we just feel that we prefer people attending our shows to focus on the clothes and not on all that is put around them in and by the media.

SF: It still helps to be thin though, doesn't it?

MM: It can be frustrating that our industry is organised in such a way that the garments manufactured for a sales collection and a fashion show are made up in a size forty-two [Italian sizing]. More often than not it is too costly and labour intensive to produce fashion show and press samples in varying sizes and so, usually, for a fashion show and later in the fashion stories in magazines, women are found to fit the clothes rather than vice versa. This, thankfully, is quite the opposite to the reality of how a collection is purchased by a store and in turn by the women who wear the clothes in daily life.

SF: Your latest show focused on favourite looks from previous collections: why did you choose to do that?

MM: To get the chance to bring ideas that we like from varying seasons forward a stage and to see how these disparate ideas could work together in a collection. Sometimes, even as late as six months after a collection has been finished and presented we can go '*@**!, why didn't we do that with that idea?!' Or in other instances there was no time to include certain ideas before the collection had to be closed at the factory. Spring/summer 1999 allowed us to revisit themes and garments in order to perfect them or present them in another way. It also allowed us to play with the garments from one season using the techniques of a later season. This is not the first time we have taken this approach to our work. For spring/summer 1989 we presented a very literal retrospective of our first ten collections, each season was represented by reproduced outfits from the collection all over-dyed in grey. The date of the original collection was painted around the neck of the model or on her arm. For spring/summer 1999, our twentieth collection, we have chosen to look back over our last ten collections in a different way.

SF: You showed in a house without using conventional lighting or backdrop – how do you feel that your show venues in general complement your clothes?

MM: We like to think more in terms of atmosphere than venue and opt more for stimulation than going against convention! We are often accused of renouncing convention yet, for us, this seems a very simplistic reaction to how we are trying to find our way to keep our job as interesting for us as we can. Most times we seek an atmosphere that complements our view on our work and the stimulation we require to continue our work.

The 'convention' of venues, catwalks and indeed fashion shows in general has changed greatly since our first shows. The mood of how a collection might be shown is changing. We needed, and continue to need, to be free to bring clothes into an atmosphere more true to how we view their life and spirit and that which stimulates us as a team. Clothing is designed to be worn. When it is worn it is seen by others from close. This is not the case with a catwalk. It is not seen at the same close quarters as in life. Clothing is as much a story of fabrics and form and, in our opinion, fabrics and details of form are best seen from close. This proximity may be attained at a show without a catwalk, and at a showroom (something many professionals of fashion are choosing to forget these days).

SF: What are your favourite pieces in the current collection?

MM: Those garments that most successfully respond to the combined demands made of them, be these demands of the wearer or of the creator.

SF: Do you prefer designing for men or women?

MM: Each poses its own questions, solutions, problems and challenges. We feel that it is as valid to choose/compare and contrast the two as it is apples and pears.

SF: Where does your Six collection come from?

MM: A number between five and seven! And also a name we have given a small group of garments that complement the principal Martin Margiela collection. This group combines linings of garments, T-shirts, woven garments, knitwear, a few accessories and some garments in denim adapted from past Martin Margiela collections (including, for a former season, more industrial versions of the painted jeans we have always had in the collection). Garments in the 'Six' group have a lower price than the other groups of the Martin Margiela collection.

SF: How are you finding designing the Hermès womenswear collection?

MM: We are very happy with our collaboration and how it is evolving. We are also happy that the Hermès customers are welcoming our work with the same open arms as the Hermès company did two years ago and continues to do so.

SF: Do you think the two collections feed into one another?

MM: We hope so as that was our intention.

SF: You seem uninterested in fashion as a trend-related industry – do trends and the reinvention of the wardrobe season after season bore you?

MM: Not always! We do not judge others in their work, yet, for us, we prefer to reflect the reality of our view on clothes in our collection. We have always had garments that we continue to propose for many seasons in a row (in some instances twelve!). It remains more important for us that someone finds their way of dressing as opposed to a way of dressing as prescribed by anyone else or an over-riding trend.

SF: Do you think fashion is an art or a craft?

MM: Fashion is a craft, a technical know-how and not, in our opinion, an art form. Each world shares an expression through creativity though through very divergent media processes.

SF: Who are the designers you most admire?

MM: Those with an authentic approach to their work.

04
ISSEY
MIYAKE

HOW WOULD YOU DESCRIBE YOUR FIRST
EXPERIENCE OF PARISIAN CULTURE?

I WAS FACED WITH THE HEAVY TRADITION THAT WAS
FRENCH HIGH SOCIETY AND FELT I COULDN'T GO
THROUGH WITH IT. I THOUGHT: 'I AM JAPANESE'. I
USED TO ESCAPE TO LONDON ONCE A MONTH TO
RELAX. THAT WAS MY PLACE. THERE WAS THE
KING'S ROAD, THE FANTASTIC BIBA STORE. THERE
WERE MUSICALS – I REMEMBER 'OLIVER!',
SHEPHERD'S PIE.

Issey Miyake
The Guardian Weekend magazine, 19 July 1997
Photography: Yasuaki Yoshinaga

Issey Miyake is standing at the entrance of the Genichiro-Inokuma Museum of Contemporary Art in Marugame, a monolithic, concrete cuboid structure that looks like the world's largest television set. The occasion is the opening of Arizona, an exhibition combining the work of Miyake, the local artist Inokuma – after whom the museum is named – and the celebrated Japanese-American sculptor Isamu Noguchi. To be precise, it's the children's opening, and, to this end, Miyake is surrounded by adoring, if nervous, boys and girls, all of them anxious to offer up gifts of appreciation. He accepts even the most humble of these with impeccable grace.

He puts his arms around the children as they approach and, one by one, holds up each present for inspection by the Miyake-clad crowd. There is an intricately painted fan, a pretty crocheted drawstring bag, a paper flower-strewn straw hat, which Miyake, grinning from ear to ear, models for the cameras. There's even a particularly lurid portrait of the designer. 'It looks more like Marcello Mastroianni to me,' says one uncharitable onlooker.

Curated by Miyake, the Arizona exhibition is of immense personal and local significance. Noguchi, who died in 1988, was part of the first generation of Japanese artists to bridge the east–west divide – he trained in Paris with Brancusi in the Twenties and later lived between America and Japan – and was to begin with an inspiration to and then a close friend of Miyake (a Noguchi sculpture takes pride of place in the courtyard of Miyake's design studio in Tokyo). Noguchi lived and worked near Marugame, and he was buried in his garden beneath a gravestone he sculpted before his death. Though his name is little known in England, Noguchi's influence nevertheless pervades thousands of households in the shape of his Akari lamps: paper copies of the collapsible, spherical version are a common fixture in bedrooms and hallways across the world.

Inokuma, whose naïve black-and-white scrawls decorate the façade of the gallery, was similarly internationalist. This exhibition focuses in particular on the sketchbooks from his travels in Arizona. His monochromatic Kachina dolls – based on those of the Hopi Indians – loom large on the gallery walls. They look like primitive robots.

Inside the museum, children run riot through the three-floor exhibition. They climb all over Noguchi's brightly painted playground sculptures, which are displayed alongside rainbow-coloured Miyake designs, finished with pointy paper hats. They gaze awestruck at Inokuma's drawings – monumental on the walls then reduced and printed on white Miyake tunics – and form spellbound clusters beneath pleated, crumpled Miyake creations that, suspended from the ceilings on lengths of elastic, bounce up and down, threatening to engulf them.

It's all a far cry from the atmosphere of grudging tolerance, or even outright disapproval, that any parent who has ever taken a child to a Western art gallery would expect. More remarkable still is that such an exhibition should take place at all in a small town such as Marugame, on Shikoku Island, off the coast of southern Japan, a place my guidebook describes as 'the last any tourist would visit'.

Phenomenally beautiful, Shikoku represents a traditional, rural side of Japan that is now threatened with extinction.

'Always people say that is art or that is design,' Miyake tells me later. 'But to show it is the same. It's a great pleasure for me to be able to do that.'

Arizona is nothing if not testimony to this. Inokuma's drawings are effortlessly transformed into pattern on clothing. Noguchi's lampshades are sweet and playful, adorning the heads of ivory-clad mannequins – Noguchi designs fold horizontally; Miyake's are pleated vertically. Laid out flat, meanwhile, Miyake's pleated garments cease to resemble clothing and become pure abstract forms instead, the perfect accompaniment to Noguchi's more serious work. Most remarkable of all, though, is that men, women and children are actively encouraged to interact with the brilliantly harmonious whole to their hearts' content.

If the show is, ultimately, a triumph of democracy over élitism, this is, of course, just what one might expect of Miyake. His collaborations with artists and architects past and present – and the predilection of his loyal following to wax lyrical about the space between the body and the garment, rather than simply the garment itself – has led to an intellectualisation of his designs that many people find unacceptable in fashion. But Miyake himself is, most of all, concerned with appealing to as wide a cross-section of people as possible. In Japan, he is a national institution. He has appeared in TV ads for beer and sake, and has even designed the clothes for the factory workers at Sony. More than anything, though, he says he wants his clothes to be enjoyed, to be 'fun', to infiltrate popular culture in much the same way as blue jeans and T-shirts have.

'I take these out because I know you smoke!' announces

Miyake gleefully, brandishing a packet of cigarettes when we meet later that day. With his sparkling black eyes, flashing white smile and seemingly poreless smooth skin, he is silent-movie-star handsome – ageless.

The gifts he had received earlier from the children are laid before him on a huge blond wood table. 'These are my treasure', he says. 'When I first came to Marugame, I noticed that even very small shops selling tofu, fish, bread, kimonos, things like that, had children's drawings of Mr Inokuma. And I remembered children and also Mr Inokuma's love of children and thought, "Why not?" Why don't I also prepare the exhibition for children? There is such a great pressure for ordinary people to get into museums. They think [he whispers] "How am I going to get into it? I must be quiet. I must learn something." But I think this is a museum of the city, a really special space. A nice space for people to be able to react. They begin to move, they begin to dance. They want to touch the exhibits. I say, "Okay, let them do it." '

It is impossible to resist attributing, at least in part, Miyake's gentle spirit to the fact that he was born in Hiroshima. On 6 August 1945, he was seven years old and cycling to school when the Americans dropped the atom bomb. By November 1945 more than 140,000 of the city's 350,000 population were dead. A further 60,000 have since died from radiation-related diseases. Miyake lost most of his family, including his mother, who, although severely burned, carried on working as a schoolteacher for four years before she died. There was no medicine. Friends treated her burns with raw eggs.

When he was 10, Miyake developed bone-marrow disease, the effects of which he suffers to this day. Otherwise, he says, 'I'd better forget', preferring to dwell on happier aspects of his childhood: a beautiful bridge in Hiroshima, which he cites as his first consciousness of design; stopping his bike to press his nose up against shop windows and admire the mannequins. 'They changed every month, those windows. I saw myself in them. I was fascinated.'

Although Miyake prefers not to talk about Hiroshima, he will, of course, never forget it. Backstage at his autumn/winter 1995 show in Paris, more than 100 assistants wore white T-shirts printed with a dove of peace to commemorate the 50th anniversary of the event. The critic Mark Holborn once wrote: 'Miyake's creativity exists not in detachment from the shadows of Japanese history,

but in an inescapable response to such experience. His career corresponds exactly to the recovery of the nation, and it is there in Japan, after both Paris and America, that his own sense of definition is established.'

At the age of 26, Miyake left Tama Art University in Tokyo with a degree in graphic design. He arrived in Paris in 1965, enrolled with the Chambre Syndicale de la Couture Parisienne and worked first with Guy Laroche, then for Givenchy, before moving to New York, where he learned about merchandising while working for Geoffrey Beene. 'I was faced with the heavy tradition that was French high society', Miyake says of his first experience in the French fashion capital, 'and felt I couldn't go through with it. I thought, "I am Japanese!" I used to escape to London once a month to relax. That was my place. There was the King's Road, the fantastic Biba store, there were musicals – I remember 'Oliver!', Shepherd's pie . . . ' And there were haircuts, he says, the best in the world.

It was to Tokyo, however, and to a country undergoing enormous cultural and economic change that Miyake returned to set up his design studio in 1970, the year of the Osaka Expo. 'Those who spent their childhood during the war years or the bleak, early days of the occupation are conspicuous as a generation', writes Holborn. 'It is as if the deprivations of the time had spurred some expansive creativity, or as if intimacy with ruins had encouraged optimism and engagement of the world.' By 1970, this creativity was burgeoning: 'The prevalent Americanisation of the occupation was replaced by the possibility of an independent Japanese culture which accommodated both native and Western traditions with a new modernity. Japan was "a nation at the height of its reconstruction under the gaze of symbols of its past". '

Although Miyake has shown in New York and Paris, and is now an international designer, he continues to live and work in Tokyo. But while his early work focused on sashiko, the quilted cotton worn by Japanese peasants, and while he has continually reinterpreted certain aspects of traditional Japanese garments, including the kimono and the fisherman's tunic, he resents being seen as a Japanese designer. His clothes are, he says, indebted to Japanese tradition, just as they are indebted to that of America, France and even England. 'I had to be free of the Occidental way, of Occidental ideas', he says, 'but there are still a lot of things to learn from them. It is very important to keep tradition.'

We are eating dinner in a tiny, deceptively unassuming restaurant in Marugame on the night of the opening of the show. The finest sashimi is served, and copious amounts of sake, always poured by the person next to you: in Japan, it is considered unlucky to serve yourself. All the women are seated around one table and the men eat and drink at the bar. As the evening continues, the feminine contingent becomes increasingly animated, until Miyake feels moved to poke his head through the curtain that separates us and shout 'very noisy women', before exploding into laughter (he does this a lot) and disappearing back to his own dinner.

In a country still famous for its chauvinism, Miyake has nevertheless always surrounded himself with 'very noisy women. Very powerful, I'm afraid,' he tells me. 'Hahahahaha.' It is the women in Miyake's life, aged from their early twenties to their late fifties, who run his company, develop his textiles, and are his closest friends. 'Because of women, I can work,' he says. 'Women are not just designers' muses. For me, women are very realistic. It is impossible for me to say that Greta Garbo is my muse. Or Diana. The women I work with always react differently to my clothes. Maybe they like this one, probably they don't like it. Then I am miserable.'

Happily, women like Miyake's clothes more often than not. Looking at the group around the table and seeing how women of all ages, sizes and nationalities interpret his designs so differently is ample evidence of his democratic sensibility at work. A short, pleated shift with platformed, wooden-soled sandals looks sweet and simple on a younger woman; the same shift, worn over pleated wide-legged pants and with a floor-sweeping coat, looks elegant, statuesque even, on another. For his autumn/winter 1995 collection, Miyake famously proved to his audience just how versatile his clothes could be by showing them on a group of women in their eighties. That the event has since been labelled, rather coolly, the 'octogenarian collection' belies the fact that the audience was visibly moved.

'I want women to be able to wear my clothes in the kitchen, when they're pregnant,' says Miyake. 'My clothes are for the young, the old, the short, the tall. They're ageless. You see?'

Ageless and entirely oblivious to passing trends, Miyake has, since the Seventies, shown alongside the likes of Sonia Rykiel, Kenzo and Karl Lagerfeld ('it was right at the beginning of prêt-à-porter. It was good: for the first-time designers were experiencing the general public'), then in the Eighties with Claude Montana and new designers such as Rei Kawakubo and Yohji. But occasional clues in hair and make-up aside, you'd be hard pushed to date his clothes, which continue to look forward and to stubbornly resist fashion, with their own, entirely original, recurrent themes.

'To change every six months,' he says, 'is crazy. It's designer suicide. And fashion design, especially now, always seems to look to the past. People must look at these ideas, see them on TV, and think, "That's interesting", but that's all. Then they forget it. We have a great evolution of industry, a lot of great new designers. They are capable of new ideas, for new centuries. Why not? If people do something new, something radical, we should applaud them. Sometimes, my clothes are radical, probably, sometimes challenging, but I try not to fear radical things.'

Certainly, people may have chosen not to wear many of Miyake's more extreme creations: bodices constructed entirely out of bamboo and rattan; waxed paper jackets with matching hats and rainbow-coloured neoprene all-in-ones, complete with neoprene knee-pads, are hardly the stuff of conventional fashion.

Perhaps for this reason, the Marugame exhibition is not the first time that Miyake has shown his clothes static. In London in 1985, at his Bodyworks show, mannequins were suspended from the ceiling over pools of glutinous black water. In 1988's A-Un (named after the unspoken Sanskrit communication between two figures either side of the entrance at a Buddhist shrine) at the Musée des Arts Decoratifs, more voluminous designs were draped around figures made out of fine, tangled wire. And in Irving Penn's photographs of his creations, Miyake's clothes are flattened, simplified into pure, geometric shapes, every trace of the human figure removed.

It is now the stuff of fashion legend that when Penn expressed an interest in collaborating with Miyake on a book, the designer simply sent 300 garments and his favourite model to New York with the message: 'Please now forget me. My work is already finished.' Equally revealing is the fact that Miyake continues to work with Penn, who to this day shoots his advertising campaigns.

But if Miyake's clothes are strangely beautiful – be they shot two-dimensionally and filling the pages of a book or set against the backdrop of the white walls of a gallery – it is, in the end, the human form and its movement that gives them meaning and brings them to full, brilliant life.

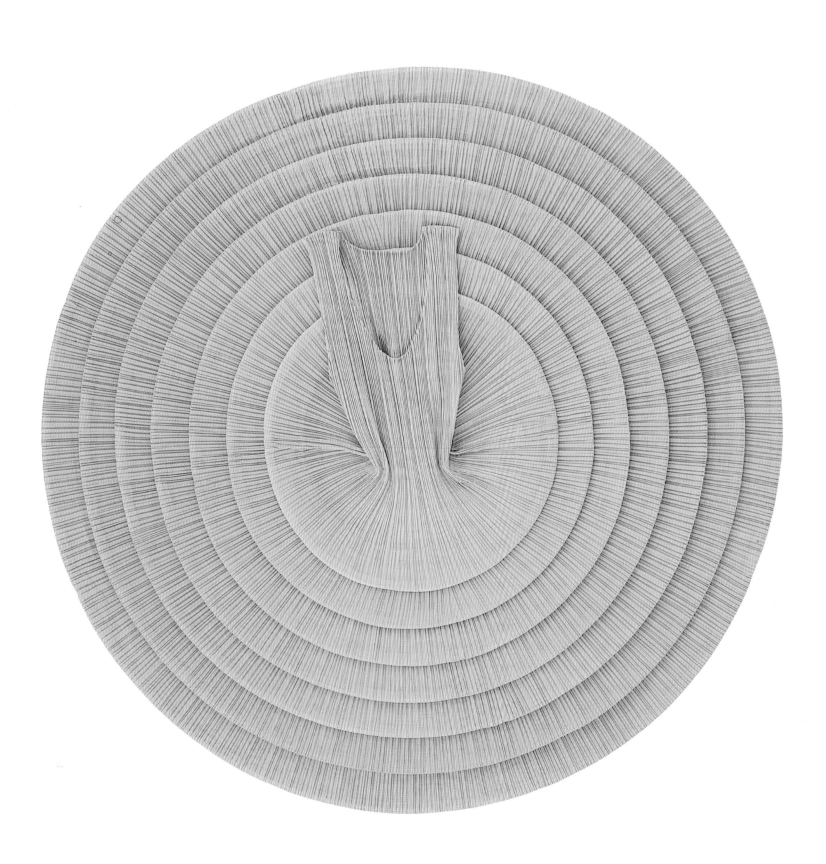

Here's how he once described his first exhibition in Tokyo, which featured a half-hour fashion show with no music but a highly sensitised sound system: 'The girl came out in many layers of clothing. She take off her shoes, throw them down. Bang! Bang! She take off garment. Ssh. She drop it on floor. Crash! She take off everything. She has no clothes. End of show. It become big Tokyo scandal. Sponsorship company beg me to stop.' By then, though, Miyake was unstoppable.

As long ago as 1976, Miyake protested against a purely Occidental concept of beauty in Issey Miyake and Twelve Black Girls – a young, suitably fearsome Grace Jones took centre stage. Today, Miyake continues to use dancers and acrobats rather than conventional models to show his work. As for the people who actually wear his designs on a daily basis: Miyake devotees claim they feel a palpable sense of relief when they put on and move in his clothes.

Issey Miyake doesn't approve of diffusion lines, which, he says, are insulting and patronising to their wearer. 'I don't want people to think of my clothes in terms of money,' he says, 'to feel they are only able to afford second best.'

It was in 1988 when Miyake first started working with pleats, and it was with the subsequent launch of the Pleats Please collection that he came up with a practical solution to everyday dress. It is here that Miyake has come closest to his dream of creating the blue jeans of the 21st century.

'My first dream,' he says, 'and why I first decided to open my studio, was that I thought to myself, "If I could one day make clothes like T-shirts and jeans, I would be very excited." But the more I worked, the more I felt so far away from doing so. I was always doing such heavy things, far away from the people. And then I was thinking, you know, "Are you stupid? Don't you remember why you started designing in the first place?" And then I thought, "Okay, Pleats Please." So I started to think how to make it, how to wash it, how to co-ordinate it, even how to pack it. And I worked on how to keep the price down.'

The Pleats Please line costs a fraction of the price of Miyake main line. Pleats – horizontal, vertical and diagonal – give the clothes elasticity and make them supremely easy to wear. Every season, Miyake adds to the collection – although it is made up mainly of classic pieces which endure. More recently, he has enlisted the work of up-and-coming photographers and printed their work on limited-edition pleated garments, using them like blank canvasses.

'For me,' he says, 'it's a very symbolic thing to change the meaning of something. Like the Walkman, for example. You know, it completely changed the idea of sound. That's great.'

So, Pleats Please becomes the Sony Walkman of designer clothing: reasonably priced, easy to care for and, most important, entirely adaptable. Women are free – indeed, they are actively encouraged – to put Pleats Please garments together in whatever way they feel suits them best. 'I make it, people take the idea and continue it. They are free to do so. To me, design must get into real life. Otherwise, it's just couture, it's just extravaganza.'

I once lent a friend who had recently had a baby some Pleats Please clothing. Her first reaction was to tell me firmly that she was in no fit state to wear designer labels. Nonetheless, I left her upstairs in her bedroom with the clothes, and half-an-hour later she emerged, flushed and triumphant, wearing one of Miyake's pleated tunics over a long, pleated skirt. She said she'd tried numerous options and settled for this combination as the one best-suited to her body shape, which in the clothes she now loved.

It is an aspect of Japanese culture that art and architecture – and for Miyake, fashion design – are an extension of nature. And so Noguchi's work embraces Miyake's, which in turn embraces Inokuma's, and the three become an integral part of a wider-reaching whole.

On Shikoku Island, local oddities include roosters with ten-metre-long tails and sumo dogs. The most remarkable thing about the place, however, is an ancient pilgrimage between 88 Buddhist temples along 1,000 miles of arduous trails. Japanese men and women in mourning carry pictures of their loved ones to these temples, some of them as often as 50 times in a lifetime. There are temples where people go to pray for their eyesight, others promising solutions for romantic problems or solace to a woman who has lost a child. From the most inaccessible temples in Shikoku – the ones frequented by only the most devout and located high in the mountains – to Takamatsu, home to Shikoku's airport, to the busy subway in the Japanese capital, people recognise the pleated garments of Issey Miyake.

'When I first started Pleats, people said it was difficult. They said, "What's that?" But to make people wonder is very important. It's a very good entrance. I like people to enjoy, to see things in a new way, but I also want them not to worry. One of the great things about being a clothing designer is that the people are free to choose for themselves.'

05
AZZEDINE ALAÏA

HOW DO YOU FEEL ABOUT TALK OF AN AZZEDINE ALAÏA REVIVAL?

SOME PEOPLE DON'T UNDERSTAND. TAKE JOURNALISTS, THEY KEEP ON ASKING ME ABOUT MY BIG COMEBACK, BUT I AM NOT BACK, BECAUSE I HAVEN'T GONE ANYWHERE. I HAVE CARRIED ON WORKING ALL ALONG. THEY DIDN'T COME TO ME. BUT THAT WAS THEIR LOSS NOT MINE.

Alaïa and Farida: Jean-Paul Goude

Azzedine Alaïa
The Independent fashion magazine, spring/summer 2001
Photography: Alex Cayley. Styling: Sophia Neophitou
All clothes Azzedine Alaïa, spring/summer 2001

Not many fashion designers cast a shadow so great that Greta Garbo comes knocking at their door. Azzedine Alaïa, however, can make such a claim.

'Garbo visited me when I was at the Rue de Bellechasse. They told me she was waiting outside with Cecile de Rothschild. I said: "Sure, who else?" And they said: "No, Azzedine, really." And there she was in a sweater, with a frightened look, her hair in a rubber band, shielding her eyes from the light with her hand, with a man's signet ring on her finger. She talked very quietly and quickly. She wanted a dark blue cashmere coat – big, bigger, biggest! And a huge collar to hide her neck.'

Garbo, of course, knew a thing or two about how to hide, and something about style too for that matter. 'She had been everybody's fantasy and, suddenly, there she was in front of me,' Alaïa explains, when invited to tell the tale once again.

When the coat was delivered, Garbo thanked him 'very sweetly', apparently, and said he had 'nice, good eyes'.

'It was quite incredible,' Alaïa says today. 'I mean, Greta Garbo is a myth.'

And such mythic stature is something Azzedine Alaïa – more than any other designer, save, perhaps, the late Cristobal Balenciaga – understands full well.

Throughout the Eighties, Alaïa was a byword for chic. Even the designer's name evoked images of exoticism, of poetry, of a decadent and extraordinary aesthete. The fact that Alaïa was not interested in marketing himself – there were no glossy advertising campaigns, no high-profile lunches, dinners or personal appearances – only added to the frisson that surrounded the name.

The supermodels loved Alaïa. Christy, Cindy, Naomi and Linda worked for him for free, in return for clothes that were the most flattering and sexy they had ever worn, thus serving to make them more famous still. It was said at the time that once a girl had worn Azzedine Alaïa anything else simply seemed too big. Certainly, Alaïa did for stretch what, many years before, Coco Chanel had done for jersey. In his more than capable hands, this medium, hitherto the preserve of swimwear – jersey, incidentally, was only used for men's underwear until Chanel got her hands on it – became the fabric to see and be seen in.

No longer did women have to suffer the discomfort of a tight-fitting tailored silhouette if they wished to show off their bodies, or eschew that look entirely and opt for a more subtle, so-called 'conceptual' Japanese/Belgium aesthetic. Instead, they could suddenly have it all. The feel of sportswear, giving and clinging in all the right places for comfort and movement, and the glamour of designer clothing, even haute couture.

Alaïa dressed women in his by-now famous bodies and leggings, his heavy viscose-knit dresses with knickers attached – fitting any other sort of underwear beneath them was, quite simply, a physical impossibility – and it seemed as if the garments had been sewn on to them, holding everything in place. These designs were more like the world's most accomplished body masks than any traditional piece of clothing. When the designer had achieved this with stretch and knitwear, he set about the even more arduous task of crafting equally sculptural clothing in woven fabric and leather, sewing it, like patchwork, in a spellbindingly complex web of near-invisible seams. This was – and remains – the ultimate second skin.

As for Alaïa's twice-yearly shows, they were, quite simply, the toast of *le tout* Paris. No matter that they tended to happen two and even three weeks late, long after the international fashion fraternity had left. Alaïa had no need for press, or even buyers to attend – the designer only ever sold to the privileged few. Perhaps because of this reluctance to promote the label – fashion wasn't yet fuelled by the mighty marketing machine that controls the industry today – little was actually known about the designer. Interviews with Alaïa were – and still are – very rare. So, was Azzedine Alaïa French or did the designer come from further afield? Was Azzedine Alaïa the man as impenetrable as the methods by which he created his clothes? Was Azzedine Alaïa really so particular that he even went so far as to iron his collection himself, where lesser designers would never deign to do such a thing? And where exactly did the umlaut on Azzedine Alaïa go again?

Azzedine Alaïa's studio is far from the grand boulevards of central Paris, home to the likes of Givenchy, Dior, Chanel et al, located instead in a tiny street in the old Jewish quarter of Le Marais. On the ground floor is a showroom, more of a gallery space than anything remotely approaching the usual designer retail experience. Clothing is exhibited – mainly in black but also in plum and all the gentle shades of green, from jade to olive – like sculpture, broken up by the odd strategically placed neat leather handbag. There is no sign of anything as mundane as a changing room. It would simply be foolish to expect any price tags. In a glass-covered courtyard, once the location of Alaïa's fashion shows, two huge German mastiffs sleep undisturbed. Upstairs, the designer lives and works with these and a veritable menagerie of further beloved cats and dogs.

I am greeted by Farida Khelfa, a strikingly beautiful woman, even by fashion standards: tall, slender, with quite the longest legs imaginable. Khelfa met Alaïa way back when, when she went to ask if she could borrow some clothes for a film of Jean-Paul Goude's. The two have been inseparable, working and holidaying together ever since.

And then Alaïa himself appears, standing at a diminutive

4ft 11in and clad in black silk Chinese pyjamas. He never wears anything else and has hundreds of pairs, apparently, explaining that any other clothes make him look ridiculously macho. He has olive skin, dense black curly hair only sprinkled with grey, and a distinctly melancholy demeanour save for twinkling dark eyes.

He is, I tell him nervously, by way of breaking the ice, in the happy position of having a fashion moment – another fashion moment, that is, of course. Austrian über designer Helmut Lang owed at least some inspiration to him in his spring/summer collection shown last autumn in New York. Elsewhere on the catwalks, designers from Lawrence Steele to Tom Ford for Gucci and from Donatella Versace to Karl Lagerfeld for Fendi more than flirted with shiny black leather, a tight-fitting silhouette, bondage and binding – all Alaïa signatures. Even Valentino, ultra-sophisticated and understated designer to the ladies-that-lunch set, sent out bondage straps. Vintage Alaïa, meanwhile, is being pulled out of the back of the wardrobes of the world's most influential stylists: Melanie Ward (creative *tour de force* at Helmut Lang) and Carine Roitfeld (editor of French *Vogue*) to name just two.

In September last year, the Guggenheim hosted an Azzedine Alaïa retrospective. More significantly for the future of the label, that same month it was announced that Patrizio Bertelli, the brash, ambitious brains behind the massive Prada empire, was forming an, on the face of it, extremely unlikely partnership with Alaïa.

'With this agreement, we wish to find a way of working in common in order to guarantee a continuity of the tradition of prestige and quality of the Maison Alaïa,' Prada stated at the time, with suitable gravitas and respect. 'Prada will start an Alaïa Foundation in Paris, which will welcome and preserve the archive of all the past and future work of Azzedine Alaïa.'

When this happens, Alaïa will become only the second ever fashion designer to have a museum opened in his name: the first, of course, being none other than the mighty Yves Saint Laurent.

'Now we are at a time when it is fashionable to recycle things,' says Alaïa, distinctly unfazed by all this attention. 'Take art, for example, or other fields. They recycle everything, create new things with what already exists. There have always been times when fashion took its inspiration from other generations. It's not very interesting. We'll just have to see what will come next.'

Speaking of the deal with Prada he is, equally, cool as the proverbial cucumber.

'My position with the group is unique, very different from that of other houses. I was interested in being part of it because Mr Bertelli made the only offer that perfectly suited my work. Others sold their name, but I didn't. I didn't want them to just throw money at me but I want them to develop things with me according to my own timing. It's a question of working with him, but the way I like it.'

Throughout the Nineties, Alaïa maintained a low profile, designing for a burgeoning number of private clients – sartorially discerning French ladies who demonstrated a rare loyalty to a man who dressed them with love and with their interests, rather than passing trends, in mind. Equally, certain buyers – at Barneys, New York, for example and, especially, at Joseph – have continued to support Alaïa, selling a tiny collection to those in the know.

Small wonder, then, that the man himself is slightly put out by talk of some sort of revival.

'Some people don't understand,' he snaps. 'Take journalists, they keep on asking me about my big comeback, but I am not back, because I haven't gone anywhere. I have carried on working all along. They didn't come to me. But that was their loss not mine.'

More surprising is the fact that, despite his status as one of fashion history's great couturiers, Alaïa seems distinctly unimpressed by the histrionics, even hysterics, normally associated with the craft. When I suggest that showing late – so late that the fashion press had left Paris – had been a brave move, fully expecting him to pour forth on the pain of creating, on the agony of his art, he says instead, very bluntly: 'When it's not ready, it's not ready. Why get stressed about it? Never mind, it doesn't matter. It doesn't mean that I am late intentionally, but if something in my life interferes with my work, let's say my dog is ill, I'd rather look after my dog than prepare a show.'

This is refreshingly pragmatic. Alaïa, it seems, is that rare thing in fashion: a well-balanced, well-rounded person, a man who appreciates the importance of clothes but also realises their place in the larger scheme of things.

'At the end of the day,' he says, 'I am the one who loses a lot for making this choice. If from the start I had wanted to make a lot of money, I would have done, like Lagerfeld, maybe even better. But I am not obsessed by fashion. There is more to life than fashion, isn't there?'

There has certainly been more to Azzedine Alaïa's life than that. His childhood is, indeed, every bit as exotic as his name would suggest. He was born in Tunis around 1940. No one knows his exact age on account of the fact that the designer says: 'Having tried hard, I forgot it.' He was brought up by his maternal grandparents. 'There wasn't a lot of money,' he once told style pundit André Leon Talley in *Interview* magazine. 'Life was poetic, lyrical. I had such a happy childhood.'

Clearly adept at playing the clown, the young Alaïa used to dance for his classmates in return for pencils, and was given more by the local midwife, Madame Pinot, whom he stayed with and assisted two days and nights a week.

He describes his first experience of childbirth thus – and it is not insignificant that he is far more animated at this point than he ever is when talking about clothes.

'Especially the first time, I was shaking. Madame Pinot was working from home and, one day, when I came in, I saw a woman lying on the table with her feet up in these things. Madame Pinot asked me to go and get some water, and I could hear the woman screaming. When I got back, I saw a head between her legs. I was petrified. That's when she slapped me to shake me up. Then she got the baby out and I watched her cut the umbilical cord.'

As well as her adept delivery skills, Madame Pinot, whose husband was a doctor, was also well versed in the arts.

'They used to have all these magazines about art galleries in Paris and books about painters like Picasso and Velasquez. I used to read them all and draw what I liked to remember. She also received a lot of fashion publications – *Vogue* and catalogues from department stores like Le Bon Marche and Samaritaine. In the evening, after work, she used to sit next to me and place orders for clothes. When the boxes came, we opened them together. I was so happy. I can still remember the little printed cotton summer dresses, the white gloves, the shoes.'

As a teenager, Alaïa enrolled at the local Ecole des Beaux Arts, where he studied sculpture: 'I was lucky to realise soon enough that I would never make a great sculptor.' Instead, on his way to school one day, Alaïa saw a sign in a dressmaker's window advertising a job finishing hems for five francs apiece and took it on the spot. From there he found his way into the hearts of 'les grandes bourgeoises' of Tunisian society, women who arranged a job for him making copies of Parisian haute couture designs ('Dior, Balmain. That's how I discovered Balenciaga. I was very interested in his work').

Before long Alaïa began designing dresses of his own, clothes of which he says today he is not particularly proud.

'It's not fair to judge people when they're very young,' he says, speaking of the new wave of young couturiers now working in Paris as well as of his own fledgling days. 'A lot of people aren't very good when they start and then later they become interesting. My work hadn't matured then but you have to go through it. It's part of the learning process. I don't even consider I'm there yet. I haven't finished.'

Through his first clients, Alaïa landed a job in Paris – at Christian Dior, no less, then presided over by its namesake, assisted by the young Yves Saint Laurent – where he worked for a grand total of five days. The Franco-Algerian war broke out and the designer didn't have the right papers. Later he spent two seasons at Guy Laroche.

'At Dior, I met Marguerite Carre,' he says, clearly, and quite endearingly, still awestruck to this day. 'She was an incredible woman, she symbolised my vision of the big

technician, people like that don't exist any more. I was all eyes. No one could understand what this young Tunisian guy like me was doing there.'

In 1960, through one of his old Tunisian contacts, Alaïa, who had been making money to survive as a designer by housekeeping, went to work for the Comtesse Nicole de Blégiers who lived in Avenue Victor Hugo. There he cooked Tunisian dishes and looked after the children. He applied himself to this, it seems, with as much enthusiasm as he did to dressmaking. Legend has it that the Comtesse once found Alaïa fully dressed in the tub, bathing the baby.

More importantly, it was through this family that Alaïa met the cream of Parisian society, among them the aforementioned Cecile de Rothschild and Greta Garbo, and designed dresses for them. Before long, his address was passed around by the kind of women who would previously have been dressed by the great French couture houses.

By the beginning of the Eighties, Alaïa's signature style of curvy, figure-hugging dresses and jackets began to take hold with a more fashion-conscious sector of society: magazine editors, artists and, finally, models, who knew more than anyone how much an Alaïa dress could do for them. And the rest, as they say, is history.

Today, Alaïa is still stocked by his loyal outlets – only four or five pieces hang in a store at any one time. Any young upstart retailers wishing to invest in his designs, meanwhile, may well be disappointed.

Ring Joseph – Joseph Ettedgui, that store's founder, is, and always has been, one of Alaïa's greatest supporters – to find out when the spring/summer Alaïa collection will be in stock, and prepare to be met with snorts of derision.

'It comes when it comes,' says a buyer. 'And we are privileged to have it.'

It seems, then, that those who care about such things will be more than happy to wait for their seasonal fix of Alaïa. Because, above all, the designer, who might not care about the foibles of the fashion industry, loves women.

'I really love it when a woman wears a new dress,' he says, 'and someone falls in love with her the same day. Imagine a woman has been working in the same office, with the same boss, for the last ten or twenty years, and one day, because she's got a new dress, the boss notices her and decides to marry her!'

Alaïa, more than any other designer, might well have the power to transform a woman. In the meantime, for less affluent souls, there's always Alaïa make-up – a future project to be taken up by the Prada group – to look forward to.

'Yes, I will be doing that,' says Alaïa happily. 'Especially lipstick. Lipstick for women to use when they kiss their loved one. A kiss from Alaïa.'

Suffice it to say that the pleasure will be all ours.

06
HUSSEIN CHALAYAN

DO YOU RESENT BEING DESCRIBED AS PRETENTIOUS?

TO CALL SOMETHING PRETENTIOUS IS THE LAZIEST THING YOU CAN DO BECAUSE IT'S JUST SO EASY. PEOPLE DON'T REMEMBER THAT WHATEVER WORK YOU DO, EVEN IF IT'S SEEN AS PRETENTIOUS, IT'S STILL WORK THAT YOU DID, AND IT'S SACRED, YOU KNOW, THE MONTHS YOU SPENT DOING THAT PROJECT. I DON'T THINK IT'S RIGHT FOR SOMEONE TO COME ALONG AND FLUSH IT DOWN THE DRAIN. IF PEOPLE COME ALONG AND SEE SOMETHING AND DON'T LIKE IT, OR DON'T TOTALLY UNDERSTAND IT, THEY SHOULD STILL SEE IT FOR WHAT IT IS AND JUDGE IT WITHIN ITS OWN DEVELOPMENT.

Portrait: Mauricio Guillen

62 i.
Hussein
Chalayan

Hussein Chalayan
The Independent fashion magazine, spring/summer 2000
Photography: Mark Aleski. Styling: Sophia Neophitou
All clothes Hussein Chalayan, spring/summer 2000

The British Fashion Awards, February 2000, and Hussein Chalayan is named British Designer of the Year for the second time. Amid all the back-slapping and self-congratulatory platitudes that habitually dominate this type of event, Chalayan's dour acceptance speech, and even his deliberately earnest body language, are a refreshing and revealing reflection of what makes him so unique.

Dressed in an immaculate black suit and black T-shirt (modern fashion doesn't do black tie), he strides up to the stage. Dispensing with the usual air-kissing histrionics, and with great seriousness, he shakes hands firmly first with presenters Graham Norton and Davina McCall, then with the chairman of the official sponsor for the evening, Rover, and then even with Naomi Campbell, a woman who's probably never shaken hands with anyone in her entire life. (Her chiselled cheekbones must be some of the most brushed in the business, after all.)

Looking more worried than happy to collect his trophy, Chalayan frowns and begins.

'I'm obviously very honoured to be given this award for the second time. I was not expecting it at all. I thought Clements Ribeiro should have won it.'

From the lips of any other designer on the planet this would sound like false modesty, a particularly transparent attempt at charming self-deprecation. Chalayan, however, is not a man famous for such social niceties. Clearly increasingly concerned, rather than gushing forth on the merits of British fashion, he goes on to vent his dismay at London Fashion Week as a whole.

'I'd like to take this opportunity to say how disappointing it was this week that all the press were still so impressed by celebrities appearing on designers' catwalks.'

Victoria Beckham, opening and closing Maria Grachvogel's catwalk presentation in a dress she had already been seen in on more than one occasion, had, of course, knocked every other designer, including Chalayan himself, off the news pages and was treated as the biggest splash of the week. For those who don't know about such things, it should be pointed out that Grachvogel is hardly a hot ticket. This was nothing more than a cheap publicity stunt. To make matters worse for the likes of Chalayan, it worked.

'I'd like to say that it was specially disappointing because that space could have been given to all the designers who bust their gut in the last week or so. It's just very sad to see that that is given to celebrities. It's Fashion Week, not Celebrity Week.'

As the entire room erupts and gets to its feet with respect for the only man in the industry ever likely to come forward and say such a thing, Chalayan, rather than basking in any unexpected added glory, looks thoroughly annoyed.

'No!' he shouts, 'I'm not saying it for applause.'

Instead, he is saying it simply because he means it, which would not normally be all that remarkable except that this is the biggest social event on the British fashion calendar and the room is filled with people hardly famous for either their gravity or sincerity. But then, over the past five years, this is the niche that Chalayan has carved for himself.

Now 29, in the seven years since he left college, Hussein Chalayan has risen slowly but surely to the top of his field, struggling all the way, even more than most, because of his refusal to compromise either his vision or his ethics. At best, he has been labelled too cerebral for his own good; at worst, pretentious. Instead of letting any such negative commentary distract him in any way from his goal, however, it has spurred him on. He is by now not only in control of his own line but also designs a twice-yearly collection for TSE New York, which goes a long way towards supporting the former. Winning the Designer of the Year Award not once but twice is nothing if not testimony to the fact that, even in the most fickle of worlds, blind determination and belief in your own abilities pay off.

'To call something pretentious is the laziest thing you can do because it's just so easy,' he says, sounding (as always) rather worried, sitting huddled over tea and hot buttered toast in a basement café in London's Covent Garden, next door to Chalayan HQ.

'People just don't remember that whatever work you do, even if it's seen as pretentious, it's still work that you did, and it's sacred, you know, the months you spent doing that project. I don't think it's right for someone to come along and flush it down the drain. If people come along and see something and don't like it, or don't totally understand it, they should still see it for what it is and judge it within its own development.'

It's not news that the British in particular are famously suspicious of anything even remotely approaching the conceptual in fashion – 'a dress is a dress' is the thinking and anything more thoughtful than that is not to be encouraged.

For Chalayan, the concept is as, if not more, important than the clothes themselves. This is particularly true of the thinking behind his twice-yearly shows, which bear greater similarity to art installation than anything remotely resembling a straightforward catwalk presentation. Past conceits have included examining the role of women in fairytales (dresses sprouting pieces of rope as a reference to Rapunzel's escape from her tower in a garment inspired by a kite), in religion (the convent girl and covered Muslim have both made an appearance), and in society as a whole (themes of isolation and oppression are continually explored).

The only child of Turkish-Cypriot parents, Chalayan was born in Nicosia in 1970. Turkish is his mother tongue.

'My mother was very dexterous, especially by Cyprus

standards. She made all my clothes and they looked like she'd bought them at the shops. Whatever she did, she did really well, and I think that sort of set the standard for me.'

As a child, the young Chalayan was very introverted.

'I spent a lot of time in Cyprus on my own but there were always things I had a real passion for. I used to love building things, creating environments was such a big thing for me. And Cyprus, you know, is a Mediterranean island so it's very colourful in some respects. It's also a divided island and I was really fascinated with the idea of it being divided. We could see the border culture, and you grow up with this fascination for what's going on on the other side, but you can't actually see it. It's such a tiny island and yet it's a separate country. I was so inspired by, or engulfed by the things I did as a child. I think they come back to me now and again, the same feelings come again and I guess I cultivate them or they influence me in one way or another. It's very subtle, but it still happens.'

A preoccupation with clothes was evident as early as the age of nine or ten.

'I was always very interested in clothes as a child. I actually made a lot more effort than I make now. I wasn't trendy or anything like that but I always loved wearing unusual colours and would wear things that nobody else would wear and have my hair different to everybody else's.'

Aged 12, and following the separation of his parents, Chalayan travelled to this country with his father who has now worked here as a restaurateur for more than thirty years. 'My father is this incredible cook. He does it better than most people. As a family we are real perfectionists and I've taken that to the point where I'm obsessed by it.'

Although he is very respectful of his father, Chalayan speaks of his mother with more love and affection than for any other person, consistently talks about the importance of women over men in his upbringing and mourns women's subordination both here and abroad.

'I have always been so interested in women,' he says, becoming unusually animated. 'I love women. I was brought up by women. In a way, it's the fact that my mother, growing up where she did, had so few opportunities, that has made me ambitious. I wanted to make the best out of any talent or any passion that I might have.'

Such impassioned views on this subject in particular may well stem from the fact that the designer clearly found being taken away from his own mother at such a formative age traumatic.

'My father didn't want me to be brought up by my stepfather. I found that separation from my mother really difficult. Although at twelve, you're quite old, you're not really, and especially those days, twelve was a kid. Nowadays children are exposed to so much more information, they're much more grown up than I was.'

It didn't help that his father chose to send him to public school, which must have proved still more of a shock to his son's already delicate system.

'I guess it's like a child's idea of the army,' he says. 'It was really horrible at first. I couldn't really speak English. You know, no one could ever pronounce my name. Children can be very cruel, more so here than in Cyprus. It's much more brutal here to be a child. I'd dread assembly in the morning when they had to read out your name. They used to make us do leapfrog around the pitch. It was really humiliating.'

The image of Chalayan as a boy, leapfrogging his way around a rugby pitch is indeed an uncomfortable one. He was, however, more resilient than to let this sort of thing crush his considerable spirit.

'I didn't look particularly foreign. I saw a lot of other kids having a much harder time. What happens is it's all so horrible you have to like each other and you sort of find a way of getting on with everyone. You know, it made me really independent.'

From school, Chalayan went on to a foundation course in the genteel town of Leamington Spa where he came up with the not-so-genteel concept of fabric printed with cuts of meat. This earned him a place at Central Saint Martins School of Art and Design where he studied for four years. Fashion legend has it that one tutor in particular told him at the time 'to bugger off and study sculpture'. He had, in fact, seriously considered following a career in architecture.

'As a child, I loved painting environments,' he says. 'I drew situations. Basically I felt that I had to do something linked to the body. Architecture was the first thing that came to mind because the essence of what's talked about – you know, the relationship between an environment and a space you create around something with its social or physical connotations – is very much what I think about. When people talk about clothes, they don't talk about clothes in the context of society, in the social or cultural context, they just take them at face value. That's not something that interests me.'

Teachers and fellow students alike reportedly found his intense arguments about religion and identity challenging, if not plain irritating. Not that Chalayan would ever let a little thing like that put him off.

'I sometimes don't like calling myself a fashion person,' he once told me. With his earnest manner, shaved head and uniform of check shirt, zip-fronted cardigan, lace-up boots and battered jeans he is far from a walking advertisement for his trade. 'I really do think I'm an ideas person. People often don't realise that whatever an idea is, ideas are always valuable. There's something to be respected in every given idea, no matter where it comes from. Of course I'm excited by clothes too, but . . . '

Chalayan first came to the public's attention when, in

1993, while still studying at Central Saint Martins, he buried his degree collection in a friend's back garden to discover how it would decompose. Since that time, he has crafted clothes in unrippable paper that can be folded into their own envelopes then sent through the post, suspended chiffon dresses from helium balloons and embellished razor-sharp tailoring with light-up flight paths. More recently, he has created special 'sets' rather than showing his collections on a humble catwalk. This usually takes the form of a bright white cube, distorted by mirrors and walls. Instead of the requisite throbbing soundtrack, Chalayan is more likely to offer up a Gregorian choir. In place of camera-friendly hair and make-up, he has been known to encase models' heads in gleaming pods of polished wood.

The true genius of Chalayan, however, and the reason why his talent has finally been acknowledged, is that for all his questioning of the conventions of fashion and need to communicate often very complex thought to his audience, the clothes themselves are breathtaking in their apparent simplicity, poetic in their purity. Despite their creator's rigorous perfectionist approach, they are also remarkably gentle on the wearer.

'It's so disappointing when people assume my clothes are difficult,' he says. 'They're not. I love seeing people in my clothes and I often do, more than many other British designers. I think it makes them seem real. My clothes should be something women wear because they like them, because they enjoy the intimate space between my clothes and their bodies. That, to me, is very important.'

And because they work: despite what is often perceived as the indulgences of the man, one of the most interesting things about him is that his clothes are anything but.

'I think that what makes something modern is its functionality, that's what modernism was created for, that the design of something comes from its function. The final result of the work is minimal, but it's not minimal in the sense that a lot of research and thought has gone into it. It's like when you refine an idea over and over again. I don't like things that are over-designed. I think you can get away with more faults when things are over-designed because you can tuck them away somehow. It's easier to create an impact with that than with something that is less. It's harder to edit an idea than it is to add on.'

Those who work with Chalayan will testify to the fact that, in the manner of the great classicists – the Balenciagas of this world and, more recently, Jean Muir – the designer will struggle for days and even weeks to eliminate a single seam. If his work is minimal, it is minimalism so full of thought and ideas that to describe it as such, thereby reducing it, in fashion terminology at least, to the level of, say, Calvin Klein, would be to insult the amount of work that has gone into each and every piece. And because of

such a concentration of work, it is hardly surprising that Chalayan is a designer whose style subtly evolves, rather than one who adheres to trends and changes his signatures season after season.

'I spend hours trying to do something,' he says, 'and how are you supposed to do that if you start trying something totally different. If you have a belief in what you do, if you have conviction, then keeping up with trends shouldn't bother you. I think you have to be really quite a weak person to be affected by that because if you base your life on what other people think and do all the time, you go mad. It's nice if people like what you're doing and they like it every season. But sometimes they don't. And that's fine too.'

With this in mind, spring/summer 2000 was something of a breakthrough for Hussein Chalayan. Perhaps for the first time, his audience did more than grudgingly accept his extraordinary talent as both a designer and showman, instead truly loving his show from start to finish on an emotional as well as purely cerebral level. Certainly, there was a lightness of spirit to the proceedings that hasn't been seen before – sugar-pink dresses that looked like candyfloss; a remote-control creation which, when operated by a nine-year-old boy, revealed an underskirt worthy of a prima ballerina and a blow-up version like the world's most glamorous ballgown/rubber ring. (His forthcoming autumn/winter collection, shown in London last month, continued this playfulness, featuring tables that transformed into dresses, and chairs into suitcases. It was widely considered to be the highlight of the week.)

I ask Hussein Chalayan whether something has happened that has made him happier, less weighed down by the challenges that his life and work throw at him. Rumour has it that the designer is in love.

'What?' he says, typically straightforward. 'So you mean I was a miserable git before. I think the collection is very feminine, and maybe lighter than my work has been for a time. I think to begin with my work was romantic and feminine. I was also very interested in concept and symbolism in relation to concept. Then I was preoccupied by technology and went on a route where I focused on that without the feminine romantic side. I think now I'm putting those things together. I don't like being stuck to one thing. I like exploring new things for myself but hopefully so it flows from my previous work. The only way you can evolve your work is by seeing it as an ongoing wheel, that's the only way I can cope with the sort of horror of transience which I really hate, I can't stand it. I think I am quite a serious person or, at least, I take things seriously – there's a difference, perhaps. I don't think I'm stern. I feel that perhaps subconsciously maybe I'm a bit more relaxed than I used to be but at the same time I'm finding things harder than ever. I learn new things all the time.'

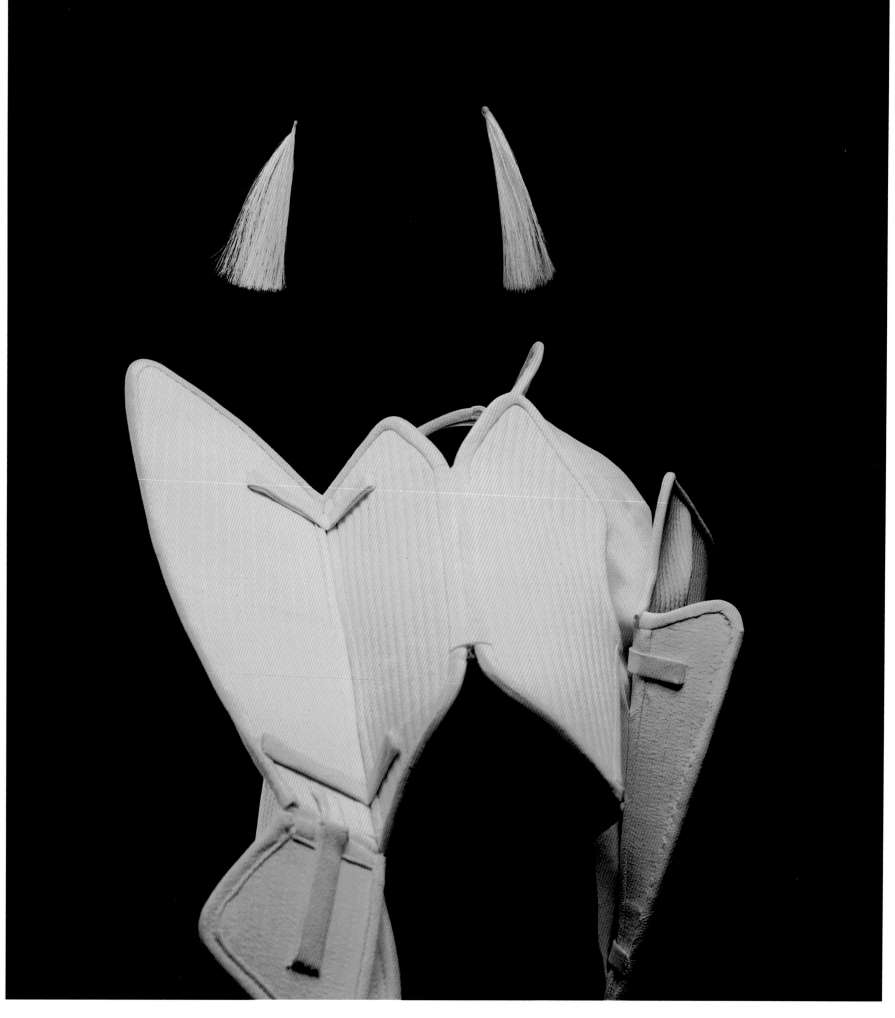

07
DOLCE & GABBANA

WHAT DO YOU THINK ABOUT WHEN YOU'RE WORKING?

WHEN WE DESIGN A DRESS WE TRY TO IMAGINE
WHETHER A MAN WILL WHISTLE AT THE WOMAN WHO
WEARS IT. IF HE WILL, IT'S OKAY.

Portrait: Gianpaolo Barbieri

Dolce & Gabbana
The Guardian Weekend magazine, 4 October 1997
Photography: Ben Ingham. Styling: Romaine Lillie
All clothes Dolce & Gabbana, autumn/winter 1997

While Italian superstar names like Armani and Versace continue to dominate the headlines, Domenico Dolce and Stefano Gabbana have been out on a limb for more than ten years, developing a hot, southern style all of their own, now honed to perfection. There's nothing self-consciously cool about the label. Instead, Dolce & Gabbana's designs are overtly romantic, unashamedly voluptuous, and women the world over love them for it.

We are having tea at Dolce & Gabbana's wildly extravagant Milan headquarters. There's a leopard-print room, a zebra-print room, and more cardinal-red draping and heavy gilt furniture than your average baroque banqueting hall. True to the bacchanalian surroundings, Dolce and Gabbana are waxing lyrical about women's breasts. It's the stuff of legend that they have a shrine to the bra in their showroom. They're positively obsessed.

'I like very much certain things,' says Dolce, dreamily. 'I like for example one bra. I sketch every season one bra.'

'It's true,' says Gabbana, interrupting his friend (he does this a lot). 'I try to stop him. I say, next season I don't want to present in a fashion show one single bra. Then, after two months, I don't know why, I miss my bra.'

Dolce says too that he can't do without pinstripe – curvy tailoring, like corseted dresses, is a signature – and that leopard print is rarely far from the forefront of his mind.

They draw inspiration from the peasant culture of southern Italy and the films of Visconti, Rossellini and Fellini. Their heroines are Sophia Loren, Anna Magnani and Gina Lollobrigida; their heroes Salvador Dali, Garcia Lorca and Rudolph Nureyev.

'We prefer southern people,' says Gabbana. 'They have more passion. What we hate is when people put up a barrier and try and hide what they feel.'

Not for them the disaffected, downbeat looks that have dominated the glossies recently. 'Many images from the magazines I don't like. I don't like the sad image, the dirty image. I think the new generation don't like this either.' Nor are they likely to jump on the Eighties-revival bandwagon, although that was the decade that they rose to fame.

'Me,' says Dolce, 'I don't like the Eighties.'

'If it's trendy or not trendy,' cuts in Gabbana, 'I don't care. We sketch everything from new each season, but it has the same feeling. This is better in the end because I have one taste. The customer comes to my shop to buy one taste, not what is trendy. Sometimes what's in fashion is good for Dolce & Gabbana, sometimes it's not. But it's better to stay a little outside. Not to try and keep up with it all. It's better to stick with your own style, otherwise, e la morte.'

Domenico Dolce, 39, and Stefano Gabbana, 34, hail from the south and north of Italy respectively. Gabbana is the extrovert – disarmingly handsome, supremely arrogant. Dolce is less obviously imposing, a whole head shorter and with huge, slightly protuberant doe eyes. The son of a Sicilian tailor, Dolce grew up in Palermo and, disenchanted with the limitations of provincial life, moved to Milan, aged 18, to study graphic design. There he met Gabbana. Finding they had more in common than just a love of clothes, the two set up business together and have been partners in real as well as fashion life ever since.

Basking in the opulent splendour of their Milan HQ, both have come a long way. There are now Dolce & Gabbana stores everywhere from Taipei to Jeddah. As well as the main lines for men and women, there's the D&G diffusion line, D&G jeans, knitwear, underwear, eyewear, accessories, soft furnishings, and fragrances for women and men.

'I remember our first show,' Dolce says. 'We did it in an apartment in Milan. We organised it ourselves without PR, without nothing. My sister and brother were on the door.'

Their big break came later when, in 1985, they were chosen as one of three up-and-coming designers to show on the official schedule in Milan. They immediately established themselves as the mavericks of Italian fashion, showing the world that there was far more to clothes than a supremely chic trouser suit or status handbag. Perhaps because of their obsession with over-sized bras, paraded for all to see, accusations of pornography were hurled and, safe in the knowledge that a touch of controversy never hurt anyone, the designers lapped it up. They continue to flout tradition and all that is deemed politically correct.

'When we design a dress,' Gabbana once told me, 'we try to imagine whether a man will whistle at the woman who wears it. If he will, it's okay.' And it's not simply chauvinistic interpretations of women that the pair play with. If one season Dolce & Gabbana sent girls down the catwalk in bras and knickers covered in ostrich feathers, then the next the same models would appear sporting heavy-duty Y-fronts or over-sized men's suits. Similarly, they think nothing of sending men out in overtly feminine designs. Dolce & Gabbana man is very much the dandy, and proud to be so.

'This is nothing to do with sexuality or being gay,' says Dolce. 'It's just that we all have this side. In Elizabethan times, men wore high heels, women had flat shoes. It's today's society that makes men and women so different.'

Dolce and Gabbana explain that, professionally at least, they are made for each other. Gabbana is the impetuous one: he sees something in a flash and wants it executed immediately. Dolce has an eye for detail, a passion for the meticulous art of tailoring.

'I 'ate tailoring,' says Gabbana.

'My personal taste and Stefano's is very different,' says Dolce. 'Stefano is very glamour.'

' "Young", is what he means,' laughs his friend. 'Him is old, very lady. At the end of the day, though, we both try and be involved in everything, but sometimes there's too much to do and that is impossible. But we always talk to each other. If I doubt anything, I call him and ask, "Please will you come here because I'm not sure about this." '

Living and working together must sometimes be a strain on their relationship. Do they argue?

'Si,' they both chime, for the first time in unison.

'Yes, it's messed-up sometimes,' adds Gabbana. 'He has one idea and I have another. Sometimes it's not exactly the same. That's when the "&" comes out.'

I ask Dolce and Gabbana if they would ever consider designing separately. They beam at each other and, for a second time together, say a resounding, 'No.'

08 VALENTINO

WOULD YOU DESCRIBE YOURSELF AS A PERFECTIONIST?

IN MY WORK, I AM EXTREMELY PRECISE. I LOVE PERFECTION. UNFORTUNATELY, I DON'T ACCEPT IT WHEN PEOPLE TELL ME, SORRY, THEY'RE LATE. I CAN'T WORK LIKE THAT. I AM VERY DEMANDING, BUT I SUCCEED.

Portrait: Mike Thomas

'I always think it's crazy to give English people tea,' announces Valentino, whose butler has just ceremoniously offered us that very same refreshment. 'We just don't know how to do it properly.' He then launches effusively into his native Italian, aimed at PR director Carlos de Souza who, sipping from a fine bone china cup, bronzed and beautiful, is about as close to radiant as it is possible for a grown man to be. 'He says I'm like an old woman, drinking tea in the afternoon,' de Souza shrugs, translating obligingly, entirely unfazed by what is clearly a regular and entirely amiable kind of outburst. 'What do I know? I'm from Brazil. I'm a banana.'

If anyone does know about such things it is, of course, Valentino. This is, after all, a designer who, for the past four decades, has dressed the world's most expensive women: from the young Elizabeth Taylor who ordered her first Valentino back in the Sixties while on the set of *Cleopatra* in Rome and wore it to the premiere of *Spartacus*, to Jackie Kennedy who married Aristotle Onassis in one of Valentino's designs – the often emulated 'Jackie O' style was created by the designer. What's more, such women are, and always have been, his friends – he entertains them with impeccable good taste and always just enough restraint on his yacht, TM Blue One, in his grand palazzo in Rome, his apartment on Madison Avenue or at his holiday homes in Capri and Gstaad.

There's not a lot anyone can tell this particular designer, then, on matters concerning etiquette. Whether he need go quite so far as to concern himself with the dos and don'ts of the serving of tea is another matter. But then this is entirely in almost obsessively perfectionist character. Fashion legend has it that Valentino has the linen drapes surrounding his four-poster bed taken down twice daily and pressed. Even as a child, it is said, he couldn't sleep at night if his tiny dressing gown wasn't folded neatly on a chair just so.

The setting is Valentino's London home in affluent Knightsbridge – or his 'London Zoo' as he apparently prefers to describe it.

'I love animals,' he enthuses, in an accent thick enough to stand a spoon up in. Sadly, however, his famous army of pugs is absent. 'My family is much bigger now because one of my leetle beetches she 'ad four puppies just one week ago and I think I'm going to keep all of them. I'm so 'appy I will be able to take them here now. Oh my God! They have tattoos everywhere my family, they have everything, to pass through your British customs.' For now, though, animals, in the form of painting and sculpture, decorating walls and every available surface – monkey, greyhounds, a particularly impressive elephant – will have to do.

'I do love many, many beautiful animals. I put them everywhere from the bottom of my stairs to the top.'

The house was decorated by Colefax & Fowler, but Valentino has introduced touches of antiquarian exotica throughout, adding opulence to the otherwise traditionally English surroundings. When the designer is in residence, every room is heavy with the scent of immaculately cut fresh flowers.

This year marks the 40th anniversary of Valentino's career as one of the world's foremost fashion designers, the darling of any society contessa worth her salt. Such women would be lost without him. How could they possibly manage without the slender little day dresses and suits he designs for them to wear to lettuce leaf lunches, the printed silks for garden parties, the little black dresses for informal dinners, the long beaded lace confections for black tie, or even the odd over-blown ballgown for gala soirées – only those rich enough to transport these by private plane need apply. The sort of woman who wears Valentino thinks nothing of spending £6,000, say, on a couture cocktail dress, even upwards of £1,000 on a little something from his ready-to-wear collection. She is – ideally – utterly refined, stands out effortlessly in a crowd, while never screaming her fashion credentials from the rooftops. She's also – it almost goes without saying – impossibly thin.

'I know women often say, "Ah, if you want an evening gown, go to Valentino," ' he tells me, referring to himself in the third person, like royalty. 'What is the point of going out if nobody notices you? Stay home! Stay home and invite some friends and you can wear what you like. But if you want to go out and be, for one evening, beautiful, with lots of seduction, sexy and everything, you must do the big number, no?'

Past 'big numbers' have included a cape in triple black silk organza worn by Audrey Hepburn in the late Sixties, a flame silk-fringed poncho and belt of coral beads worn by Grace Kelly at the Bal de la Rose in Monaco, and an aquamarine satin toga dress, edged with silver and rhinestone embroidery, worn by Jackie Kennedy for an official visit to Cambodia in 1967 – Valentino designed her entire wardrobe for the tour. Perhaps Valentino's greatest gift to fashion is his ability to pile everything but the kitchen sink onto a garment – beading, lace, embroidery and over-embroidery – while ensuring that the end result is as light as a feather.

'I 'ave to tell you,' he tells me, 'I worked from the Sixties to the Nineties, okay. If I think about my whole lifetime and going through my whole archive, the Sixties were really something. We had the most beautiful women – Marie

Agnelli, Dolores Guinness, Jackie Kennedy, she was somebody so important for me. All those beauties, they were really at home with elegance and beauty, always so perfect. During that period, we didn't have any ready-to-wear, just high fashion. So the very important ladies around the world, they used to dress in high fashion. All the short skirts, the boots, small girls. The Sixties, for me, was quite a good decade. It was extremely sophisticated. But, you know, women, they didn't move one finger. They were all wearing this huge, beautiful hair. They were all made up, beautiful eyes and everything. The dresses were beautiful, all the little dresses, beautiful pyjamas.'

He continues, running through the years blithely, seemingly unaware that he is delivering – without obvious ceremony – a considerable slice of fashion history.

'After, we jump to the Seventies. There was liberation, women, they want to have curls, they want to be made up in a different way, to be more free, to wear tight clothes.' He outlines the clothes with fast and furious hand movements as he speaks in short, sharp sentences. 'Jacket – fur around. Shirt – ruffles. Big trousers – low waist. If I think of the most amusing decade, it was the Seventies.'

Almost as if catching himself revelling in nostalgia and realising, not unreasonably, that he'd rather not be buried in the archives, Valentino, without batting a well-mannered eyelid, suddenly fast forwards to the present.

'I realise lately that fashion has changed a lot. I try now to make it extremely pleasurable, extremely good quality, but everything is more relaxed, more subtle. In the past, never would you imagine taking a jacket from the haute couture and wearing it with a pair of jeans. But it's very chic. You know, if I think of today, I love young people. I love young, beautiful girls. It is a pleasure to see them in my clothes. If you take women today you have . . . They are different . . . They are more . . . Maybe not voluptuous, no. Not sensuous, no. But more with . . . With guts! Take, for instance, Julia Roberts. She is amazing. Full of life. Take Cameron Diaz. These are the new icons. They have another look, another way to live. They are more concerned about business, about doing two thousand things in one minute. Before, those ladies, they did charities and things but life was smooth. Now the young generation can fight for anything. They are not waiting to be bought things by their husbands. They buy them themselves. This is fantastic! I accept this because I go on and on and on and I don't want people to mention that Mr Valentino is attached to the past and has no concept of what is fashion today.'

Last January, for his spring/summer haute couture collection, Valentino drew on references from his own considerable back catalogue to celebrate his anniversary:

there were the neat little Jackie O shift dress and coat combinations in ivory and, of course, bright Valentino red – he is to that colour what Schiaparelli was to pink. There was a peach silk poncho. There were fluid, wide-legged trousers and fine chiffon blouses with waterfall collars; silk column dresses that plunged revealing slender backs. The little black dress came in all shapes and sizes – slim as a pencil, narrow to the hips, then with a flirtatious flippy skirt, empire line or drop-waisted. There was lace – black embroidered with white, white embroidered with black. It was an unashamed collection of greatest hits, bringing a smile to even the most hardened fashion editors' lips.

The twice-yearly haute couture collections in Paris may have become a media circus, attended by film and TV crews and some 2,000 journalists as well as the well-heeled couture customer, but Valentino's show, which always takes place early evening, remains a quieter, more formal occasion. The women wear Valentino cocktail dresses from the previous season, the men change into dark suits and freshly pressed shirts for the duration.

'Of course, I refer to my own designs but, with my eyes of today, everything can be even more beautiful. Maybe I adjust just a little bit the proportion, because when you copy and it's exactly the same, it doesn't work. You must have enough ability, enough experience, to do a Marie Antoinette crinoline but make it for today, in a different way, you understand?'

He was born Valentino Clemente Ludovico Garavani on 11 May 1932 in Voghera, a small town between Milan and Turin in the north of Italy. His father presided over the local electrical supplies store.

'I think I always wanted to work in fashion,' says Valentino. 'When I was a young boy I was fascinated. My sister, she used to take me, without my parents' permission, to see films. I went to see films when I was thirteen – that's like five today. I was fascinated to see the old movies of the silver screen, to see Lana Turner and Katherine Hepburn. And I dreamt about it. So I started doing fashion drawings without having any idea how to make fashion drawings.'

He learned the craft proper when, in 1949, he enrolled on a fashion sketching course at the Santa Marta Institute in Milan. At the same time, he took a course in French before moving to Paris a year later to study at the school run by the Chambre Syndicale de la Couture Parisienne. While still a student, Valentino won a competition for fashion design sponsored and run by the International Wool Secretariat – both Yves Saint Laurent and Karl Lagerfeld later won the same prize.

From there he went to work at the couture house of Jean Desses, then, in 1957, at Guy Laroche. In 1960, backed by his father, Valentino opened the house bearing his name.

From the start, his partner was Giancarlo Giametti, a former architecture student who fiercely protected the young designer and, taking over the business arm of the label, allowed Valentino to concentrate on what he did best. Giametti is widely considered to be one of the toughest businessmen in international fashion – the relationship between himself and Valentino is often compared to that of Pierre Bergé and Yves Saint Laurent. He remains by the designer's side to this day.

Almost two years ago now, amid a blaze of publicity, Valentino and Giametti sold their empire – which now includes haute couture men's and women's ready-to-wear lines, accessory and home collections as well as lucrative fragrances – to Holding di Partecipazioni Industriali (HdP). This was just one of a number of business deals in Italian fashion that has seen a shift away from the family business to more corporate, global concerns, a shift which affects the likes of Valentino – who has no heir – in particular. He continues to design his collections for HdP, however, and is the figurehead of the label. All in all, he says, nothing much has changed.

'No, no. It hasn't been difficult at all,' he says. 'You know, I have Mr Giametti close to me. He did a lot to make my name and, of course, he did the most important thing, he always left me alone with my job without other things to think about. This means that I can work peacefully, in my creative office, do my collection, see my fabrics, my embroideries, discuss with my people. Today, we have sold my business but I am still there. I haven't changed anything.' He searches for the words to explain his position, then announces with something of a flourish: 'They keep me like a gold bird beneath a crystal bell.'

It's a curious image and one that places the designer firmly in an ivory tower of his own and Giametti's making. But if Valentino's working practices might remain the same, the industry of which he is still a part has changed immeasurably. The marketing of clothes, in particular, now often seems as, if not more important than the clothes themselves. Designers, meanwhile, must be adept in this side of things to keep afloat and are, all too often, used by big business as mere lucrative PR tools. With Giametti at his side, Valentino continues to turn a deliberately and resolutely blind eye where such banalities are concerned. Interviews with the designer are rare.

'I'm not going to put my hand in the fire,' he says, 'but there are lots of young people who do this job and they are not really designers. There are lots of designers now who are not even able to pick up a pencil and draw. You need to be able to draw. How else will you express yourself? You do a small skirt' – he draws in the air, fast as lightning – 'a sexy skirt. You do a profile, you make the arse of the girl, you make everything you want, the big shoulders, the small shoulders, you do everything, I design everything myself.'

And that everything must always be designed to perfection.

'In my work,' he says, 'I am extremely precise. I love perfection. Unfortunately, I don't accept it when people tell me, sorry, they're late. I can't work like that. I am very demanding, but I succeed and the people around me have been with me for so long.'

Now aged 68, Valentino continues to work from Rome as he always has done. This is a considerable achievement given that he shows in Paris and, while maintaining his distance, far away from the histrionics and bitching, is entirely accepted by the French fashion establishment. He says that he is simply not interested in passing trends but – and this is always the mark of a true designer – would rather develop what he does best.

'No, no. I am not trendy. You have to put these two things in two different boxes. Trendy is for extremely young people and also for people who are maybe a little bit fashion victim. What I try to do is a young collection – glamorous, sexy, extremely feminine – but not clothes that only last for a short, short season.'

Experience has also taught the designer that if you remain true to your signature, the cyclical nature of fashion means that, from time to time, the world will come round to your way of thinking once more and so, as well as catering to your core clientele, the women in a designer's life who never go away, you will attract a younger, more obviously fashionable customer.

This season the bourgeoise – she of the pencil skirt, blouse and court shoe – looms large in the collective fashion consciousness. Valentino is therefore in his element.

'I am very proud when I see young girls wearing my designs. And, you know, more and more, the young women come and they want to wear the dresses of Valentino. And you know why? If you remember, we went through grunge. Then came beeg, beeg, minimalisima. But now,' and he says this clearly with relish, 'fashion is back to beauty! Because the young people, they like to wear those clothes. They start out with this sort of complex, they don't want to be seen too much, they dress almost like nuns, with army shoes, with black everywhere. But now, suddenly, they realise that the dresses of their mothers, the vintage dresses, they are so beautiful. And they look at all the workmanship and they are really fascinated. So this makes me very, very 'appy. Because the young, they discover beauty again.'

09 HELMUT LANG

WHAT IS YOUR FAVOURITE PLACE IN THE WORLD?

MY BED.

Portrait: Elfie Semotan

Helmut Lang
From an interview with Helmut Lang for the Victoria & Albert Museum, April 2001
Pictures first published in the Independent Saturday magazine, 12 May 2001
Photography: Justin Smith. Styling: Sophia Neophitou
All clothes Helmut Lang, spring/summer 2001

My initiation into the world of Helmut Lang came during the Milan season back in the spring of 1996.

With the autumn collections in full swing, myself and the (then) fashion editor of *The Observer*, Karl Plewka, skipped lunch to nip into the newly-opened, super-minimal Lang boutique; so new there were no doors on the changing rooms at the time. Nonetheless, we dutifully tore off our clothes and set about trying on practically everything in the shop. Mr Lang was quite the most fashionable name in the Italian clothing capital, and this despite the fact that he chose to show in Paris. Humiliating ourselves in public for the sake of fashion therefore seemed quite the thing to do.

'Great baaaadies!' exclaimed Polly Mellen, a fashion legend and long-time Lang devotee, also, as it happened, in attendance, charitably ignoring the sight of our not-so-great underwear.

My friend Karl snapped up a skinny T-shirt, so shiny, long and lean it was slightly nasty in effect. This is very Helmut Lang. I, meanwhile, chose a little knee-length black dress, perfectly simple, in lightweight stretch fabric with a tiny zip at the back of the neck and two tell-tale splits at the elbow. This last small but highly idiosyncratic touch was a Lang signature at the time, speaking volumes to everyone who was anyone in fashion and inciting just the right amount of awe and/or curiosity in anyone else. That didn't stop the *Saturday Telegraph* magazine running a picture of Kylie Minogue in the same outfit and crediting it to Gucci. Or even less fashion literate souls still pointing out to me that, actually, I had not one but two dirty great holes in my dress.

When it comes to sheer urban cool, no other designer does it quite like Lang. His highly functional, immaculately finished and effortlessly androgynous designs are some of the most intelligent, understated and desirable in fashion. This is perhaps why his mean trouser suits for men and women, low-slung dirty denim jeans and cute if knowing dresses have been among the most copied designer clothing of recent years. You simply can't do better than Lang's trademark sleek and supremely flattering trousers, slim stretch tops and the best knee-length overcoats in the business. High-street chains the world over continue to be informed by this designer's aesthetic, perhaps above any other. But, and herein lies the key, the people who buy the cheap copies of Lang's designs will, more often than not, have no idea where the inspiration for their purchases originally came from.

This is not usually the case with designer labels. When a young woman buys a Gucci or Prada spin-off – the belt, shoes, pair of trousers, of the season – chances are she's seen the real version on the back of everyone from Victoria Beckham to Kate Moss. Indeed, that's why she wants it. When she buys a Helmut Lang copy, however, she loves it to bits, wears it to death, and all without ever realising that the man responsible for her clothes is in New York, working on his next great collection which will, no doubt, also find its way into her wardrobe six months down the line.

That is not to say that Lang's own customer, one prepared to spend rather more on his or her clothing than the high-street consumer, will not feel the need to continue investing in his handiwork. With Lang, over and above perhaps any other contemporary designer, the devil, as they say, is in the detail, both in the highly polished finish of a garment – a fabric loop for the button of a back pocket on a pair of trousers, say – and in the more offbeat, even whimsical, surface elaboration which is so distinctly his in flavour. There have been the aforementioned splits at the elbow, and later, shoulder, but more recently circular cutouts at the sides of trousers and dresses, and coats punched with holes. What's more, over the years, the fabrics Lang has chosen to work with have become increasingly luxurious, if never obviously so, and the technology behind the creation of supremely lightweight clothing more advanced than is possible for more reasonably priced clothing.

Despite the fact that Lang's clothing may seem deceptively simple, his name is quoted alongside the great avant-garde designers of our time – Rei Kawakubo of Comme des Garçons, Martin Margiela – as opposed to more mainstream brands. This is perhaps because, the idiosyncrasies of his designs aside, even his showing environment demonstrates a more modern and even radical spirit at play than is usual: mainly black clothes are presented against a plain, white background and on suitably slouchy male and female models. Yes, for designer ready-to-wear this is, indeed, quite revolutionary. Lang has since spawned many imitators, from Tom Ford to Alexander McQueen, who throw the odd man into the womenswear mix, safe in the knowledge that unisex really is more contemporary in flavour.

Helmut Lang was born in Vienna in 1956. Following the divorce of his parents – his mother died not long afterwards – he went to live with his maternal grandparents in Ramsau am Dachstein in the Austrian Alps. His grandfather was a shoemaker. Lang told John Seabrook in *The New Yorker* last year: 'In the mountains there was a very elegant way about basic necessities, a great beauty in a certain way that is completely refined but not about money . . . People who grow up in the city don't have that sense of taste, they don't experience it as connected to real life and nature as I did.' Aged ten, Lang returned to Vienna, to live with his father who had since remarried. It was not a happy time for the young man, whose stepmother openly disliked him, so much so that, immediately on turning 18, he told his parents he was leaving and never saw either of them again.

At around the same time, he began designing his own clothes: a certain cut of T-shirt that he couldn't find in the stores, a pair of trousers. When friends began admiring his casual designs, he set about experimenting with more formal clothes. These were an equal success, and it wasn't long before he hired a handful of seamstresses and opened a made-to-measure store. And the rest, as they say, is fashion history.

In 1997, Helmut Lang moved his business from Paris to New York, and in 1999 he entered into a lucrative

partnership with Prada, selling a 51 per cent stake in his business to the Italian fashion conglomerate. With fragrance and accessory lines now available the world over, Helmut Lang is, without doubt, no longer simply a designer but a full-on global brand.

The man himself, however, now 45, continues to maintain a studiously low profile, even accused in the past by the American fashion establishment, one almost hysterically prone to the requisite public appearance, of rudeness. He famously declined to attend the American Fashion Designers 2000 Award Ceremony, the most prestigious in the world, where he was nominated for womenswear, menswear and accessories – an accolade never before bestowed on any other designer. Anna Wintour, the formidable editor-in-chief of American *Vogue*, said at the time: 'If he had been out of the country, but he was just downtown . . .', words which would strike terror into a lesser designer's fashionable soul. Lang was honoured with the award for menswear nonetheless. For his part, Lang has since expressed a horror for such social niceties, preferring instead to get on with the job of designing, which is, after all, what he is there for. Equally self-effacing are his twice-yearly ad campaigns, displaying neither the requisite models draped, bored and beautiful, in his designs, nor his own intelligently handsome face. Instead, simply the words 'Helmut Lang' appear – a quietly confident move if ever there was one.

For his spring/summer 2001 collection, Lang presented his usual and eminently desirable signatures, while also demonstrating a more overtly sexy aesthetic. Leather bandage dresses in particular made for some of the most photographed and attention-seeking designs of the season. This is unusual for Lang, who generally prefers a more restrained aesthetic, although these garments too were instilled with a hard-edged modernity that is all his own.

And the inspiration behind such uncharacteristic audacity?

'Melanie's [Ward – Lang's creative director] boobs and microscopic natural history.'

SF: How do you like being based in New York?
HL: I felt at home immediately. I still love it every day.
SF: What is the main difference between showing in New York and showing in Paris?
HL: For me there is absolutely no difference, except that I find it less stressful showing in New York. I think New York is a more relaxed showing environment. We might show in Paris next season and in the future show between the two cities.
SF: Does it bother you that the New York collections are rarely perceived as directional?
HL: No, I just care about what I am doing and I think we are doing very well.
SF: What do you like best about New York?
HL: The directness of the people and the multi-cultural mix, the co-existence of the big and the small and the feeling that it is very alive.

SF: What do you miss most about Vienna?
HL: Nothing really. I miss my friends but they visit New York regularly anyway.
SF: Do you think your background has formed your aesthetic?
HL: Very much so. I think the simplicity of growing up in the mountains and the opulence and intellect of Vienna are two important elements of my basis structure.
SF: Have you felt compromised at all by the transition from being a relatively small label to becoming a brand?
HL: No, not at all. It has actually helped progress my work and collections, and opened new opportunities while maintaining complete integrity and quality.
SF: Does it bother you that the fashion mainstream plagiarises your ideas?
HL: Yes it does but I suppose this is what happens when you are an influential designer.
SF: What is the best thing you have ever designed?
HL: Everything – except for the first five years.
SF: And the worst?
HL: The first five years.
SF: What is the most difficult thing you've ever had to do?
HL: Go on stage and receive an award.
SF: Is black still the most flattering colour?
HL: It's the most elegant colour.
SF: Is androgyny the most modern interpretation of women's dress?
HL: Androgyny is an idea from the past. Women are feminine in many different ways. Maybe the biggest achievement of the last years is that there are many more attitudes of being a woman.
SF: Is gender important?
HL: Yes, especially for nature and separate toilets.
SF: Would you describe yourself as a conventional person?
HL: No, not at all.
SF: What has been your darkest moment?
HL: Being in a car crash in Italy before Christmas.
SF: What makes you happiest?
HL: Inner peace.
SF: How would you like to be thought of?
HL: Too early to tell, I'm still working on it.
SF: What's your favourite film?
HL: An old Austrian comedy called *Rosen in Tirol*.
SF: And your favourite book?
HL: All my books.
SF: And your favourite painting?
HL: Everything from Louise Bourgeois and Kurt Kocherscheidt.
SF: And your favourite TV programme?
HL: I love really trashy American television.
SF: And your favourite magazine?
HL: *National Geographic*.
SF: And your favourite person?
HL: That's my secret.
SF: And what is your favourite place in the world?
HL: My bed.

10
VIVIENNE WESTWOOD

WOULD YOU CONSIDER YOURSELF ÉLITIST?

WE'RE LIKE BIRDS, YOU KNOW. THE PEACOCKS DON'T MIX WITH THE HAWKS, THE SPARROWS DON'T MIX WITH THE WRENS… THE QUESTION IS NOT WHETHER I'M BEING ÉLITIST. THE QUESTION IS WHETHER BEING ÉLITIST IS POLITICALLY UNSOUND.

Portrait: James Hunkin

Vivienne Westwood
The Guardian Weekend magazine, 22 February 1997
Photography: Jane McLeish. Styling: Lucy Ewing
All clothes Vivienne Westwood, spring/summer 1997

'Now then, I was in the National Gallery the other day, in the room that's got the Van Dyke in it. And there was this Flemish or Belgian painter, I don't remember his name. Anyway, it was this painting of Elizabeth Stuart, Queen of Bohemia, and she's painted as a widow, and it's really, really stunning. She's not a pretty woman at all, but her dress is incredible. And she's got these enormous tear-drop-shaped pearls, the size of a pigeon egg I expect, three on each ear, and a wonderful pearl necklace, pearls the size of marbles going round her neck. And it says on the little plaque next to it that she's wearing very simplified clothes because she's in mourning, but she looks incredible!

'Now, I can date that painting. I can tell by the dress that it's like 1638. And I'm not saying that knowing somebody's story is the way to look at a painting, but sometimes it is a key to starting to get involved. And so the story is that Elizabeth was married to an elector of the palatinate and he was given the throne of Bohemia, which is now Czechoslovakia. And the Holy Roman Emperor didn't want Bohemia to be Protestant, so he invaded it, took it over and kicked Elizabeth's husband out. There were another couple of incidents. Somebody threw some Austrian representatives out of a window first as well, which aggravated the emperor I expect. But anyway, the emperor moved in there and they were forever in exile after that.

'But the point is that this started the Thirty Years War. There's never been a more terrible war in the history of civilisation, perhaps, than that war. Of course, the world wars were bigger in scale, obviously. But people were going over that country for thirty years and you can imagine a mercenary soldier of fourteen or fifteen who would have finished when he was forty-five. And what happened with those armies is . . . '

Vivienne Westwood is on a roll. An impossibly elliptical, entirely unstoppable roll – all quintessentially Westwood in flavour. Ask her the most innocuous question – why she likes London, for example – and don't be surprised if you are offered the history of the Thirty Years War in reply – well, you would be, wouldn't you? It's Westwood's own peculiar version of the Thirty Years War, of course, comprising impressionistic snatches of history, politics, literature, art and, quite touchingly, human interest, all rolled into one, snatched from the books she reads constantly in a seemingly insatiable effort to educate herself. ('Now then, about Proust . . . '; 'Bertrand Russell once said . . . ') Ask her whether she thinks fashion can ever be art and she'll deliver her views on the French Revolution, which, in turn, leads into her thesis on the difference between herself and her husband of five years, her former student Andreas Kronthaler.

'No, I don't think it's art. That is to say, sometimes I do. Now then, what am I trying to say? The French are the inheritors of the greatest Western thought. It didn't happen in England for various reasons. One of the main reasons was the French Revolution, the English are scared of that, and they're right. If you think too much, you have a completely anarchical society, you know. Er, sorry, I haven't said that very well. Anyway, the biggest indication of the difference between myself and Andreas is that I was absolutely upset when I heard about the French Revolution and these people going to the guillotine and how terrible it all was, and he cried because he heard about them destroying all the works of art!'

At any given time Westwood has at least two, maybe three ideas, or even sentences, on the go concurrently, uttered in hushed Derbyshire tones that career and collide until they either explode into meaning, often minutes and even hours later, or at times peter out entirely, leaving anyone who's interested to fill in the gaps. She sounds like a character in an Alan Bennett play, which only adds to the impression of naivety. A cousin of hers says that Westwood comes from a large family of women – a formidable army of cousins and aunties – all of whom conduct themselves in the same way, each then, presumably, taking the country by storm, though Vivienne is the only obvious star.

As she talks, she tugs at her (Vivienne Westwood) tweed pencil skirt nervously, chainsmokes Gitanes and struggles breathlessly to find the right words, her clear blue eyes widening, her familiar mass of peroxide blonde tufts and curls and frail body positively quivering with excitement at the endless stream of consciousness that seems to surprise even her. It is no wonder, then, that she is at times overcome, at a loss to keep up with the dizzying scale of it all. 'Sorry, I know I've waffled on. Now, where was I?'

For the autumn/winter '97 season, Vivienne Westwood, the undisputed grande dame of British fashion, returns, in all her glory, to open London Fashion Week after an absence of six years. She will be showing her diffusion line, or Red Label, in the British fashion capital. Her more expensive Gold Label, described, in her own words, as 'demi-couture', will continue to be shown in Paris. She is very happy to be taking to the London catwalk again, she says, and more than a little impressed by the work of the British Fashion Council which, in its successful endeavours to promote young British designers, has made London Fashion Week a very different, far more high-profile affair than it was last time Westwood was in attendance.

Westwood's business, too, has changed beyond all recognition. When, in 1993, she moved the production of her Red Label to the hotbed of technological genius that is the clothing industry in Italy, Westwood achieved, for the first time, mass production of a quality she was satisfied with. The Gold Label continues to be manufactured in England, often in very small factories, but it was the Italian operation that enabled Westwood to expand her business to the £20-million-per-annum concern of today. As well as the Red and Gold Labels, there's Vivienne Westwood Man ('Man can mean homo sapiens; I do it in this megalithic stone writing') and, more recently, a deal was signed with Lancaster for the first Vivienne Westwood fragrance: Boudoir.

'For years I struggled to manufacture in England,' she says, 'and the breakthrough came for me when I finally started to produce in Italy, because before that I could never really overcome the problem of production in high enough quantities. The gap between cottage industry, which is where I started and where a lot of other people started in England, and the kind of people who produce for Marks & Spencer is an unbridgeable chasm, actually. There still isn't the infrastructure or the mentality to help anybody mass-manufacture from a creative point in England.'

The Red Label appeals to her younger market, which makes it particularly suited to London, she says. More important, though, despite constant references to the fact that the French are by far the most superior nation where culture is concerned ('It's one of the tragedies of history that the British won the battle of the colonies and the world became English-speaking, because if it had become French-speaking . . . '), Vivienne Westwood, Living National Treasure, is at home here.

'I just think it's something to do with the fact that I've lived here for so long. I was born in the country, and I still live on Clapham Common. I love the changing seasons and the cold, moist air. I don't know. I get home and the Common hits me and I smell something and I think, ooooh, the elderberry's in blossom. You just have a way of life here.'

Here she goes again.

'I had a wonderful day two weeks ago. I went to see the Kirov Ballet and the thing that struck me about this ballet was this ballerina. Actually, I want to get in touch with this woman because I've never seen any woman more beautiful, no more beautiful creature in my life. She was honey blonde and she had orangey lipstick and a big mouth and big slanty eyes and she smiled all the time, for seven minutes or something, and there were these constant pirouettes and every time she turned there was this smile there all the time. And I happened to be on my bicycle, so I got there a bit early and went to the National Gallery, then went to the ballet. And I'd already arranged to meet some friends at the theatre, at the Barbican, so I went to the theatre and saw a play by Molière that was very good actually. So, in between, I was riding my bicycle down all these little alleys round Saint Paul's, doing a bit of reconnoitering, and then went to the Barbican and then, coming home, I just put my bike in a taxi. Cab drivers are brilliant. I've never been told I couldn't put my bike in a taxi in all the time I've been here!'

If Westwood 'doing a bit of reconnoitering' on her bike around London must truly be a sight for sore eyes – she certainly paints a rather quaint and eccentric picture of her life these days – it is all the more endearing in light of the fact that she is, with Yves Saint Laurent, probably the most influential fashion designer of the latter part of this century. It was, after all, Westwood who gave us not only the uniform of Punk, but also Pirates (1979–1981), which triggered the New Romantic movement, followed by Savages (1982), Western fashion's first foray into asymmetric layering, and Buffalo Girls (also 1982), inspired by the Latin American Indians and featuring layered skirts and petticoats, bowler hats worn with head scarves and, most significantly, bras worn over blouses. Madonna's now legendary conical bra, created by Jean Paul Gaultier and worn throughout her Blonde Ambition tour nearly ten years later, would never have happened if it hadn't been for Westwood playing with the concept of underwear as outerwear some time before him.

Later – when the shoulder-pad was at the height of its thrusting popularity – Westwood placed the emphasis firmly back on the hips with the mini-crini; then there were twinsets and pearls for men, the reintroduction of Harris Tweed into fashion's vocabulary, and even her very own tartan.

'It normally takes two hundred years to have a tartan recognised by Lochcarron,' Westwood's printed biography reads, proudly. 'Vivienne created her own tartan for Anglomania [autumn/winter 1993/94] and invented her own clan.' Said tartan is now displayed alongside all the others in the Lochcarron Museum. And the name of the clan? Mac Andreas, in honour of her husband, sweetly enough.

Vivienne Westwood was born Vivienne Isabel Swire in Glossop, Derbyshire, on 8 April 1941. Her father came from a long line of cobblers, her mother worked in the local cotton mills.

'I lived very much in the part of the country that had grown up in the Industrial Revolution,' she says. 'I didn't even know about art galleries until I was seventeen. I'd never seen an art book, I'd never been to the theatre or anything like that. But I could sense from a very early age that I was less conservative than my parents.' Perhaps because of this, Westwood tended to side with the underdog, although she was popular herself, and, it has to be said, not entirely modest. 'I was an attractive child to other children. I was adventurous and high-spirited and clever. I always had friends when I was little.

'I've always had a sense of justice, and I was like this little fighter when I was little, I wouldn't let people be attacked. I remember one time this poor, dirty little boy. I used to watch him sort of dancing in a little circle on his own in the playground and there was always a lot of space around him because he really smelt terrible, poor little thing. And

he was quite a pretty little boy, but he never spoke and he was very retarded because nobody ever . . . well, it was the way he was brought up. And I felt really sorry for him and told everybody that he was my boyfriend and, of course, that was the worst thing I could have done. He was so embarrassed! I made his life a misery!'

When she was 17, her parents bought a post office and moved south to Harrow in Middlesex. After working in a factory for a short while, Westwood went to teacher-training college and taught for a year ('I always liked the naughty ones') before marrying Derek Westwood and having her first child, Ben. The marriage lasted three years, with Westwood continuing to teach while making her own jewellery, which she sold on a stall in Portobello Road.

At around this time she met Malcolm McLaren, then Malcolm Edwards, and became pregnant with her second son, Joseph (who now runs chic Soho underwear outlet Agent Provocateur with his wife, Serena Rees). Westwood carried on teaching until, in 1971, McLaren decided to open a shop and she knew she could fill it. 'I wanted to read and I was intending to go to university, but I started to help Malcolm,' she says.

More than 25 years on, Vivienne Westwood has an OBE. She famously twirled knickerless outside Buckingham Palace after receiving the award ('the English aristocracy is now only the middle class with knobs on'). But while her business continues to prosper, it isn't quite so ferociously fashionable to like Vivienne Westwood as it once was.

Last year, although she was rumoured to have been approached by Christian Dior, the job went to John Galliano, almost 20 years her junior. Her press officer warned that the subject was taboo, but other than pointing out that 'we sell a lot more clothes than Dior in this country, actually' (she laughs when she says this), Westwood seems unfazed.

She's right not to care. While Galliano and Alexander McQueen may be today's fashion favourites, Westwood paved their way. Her spring/summer show revealed her to be, once again, on a high. A tribute to the flirt, Vive La Bagatelle featured push-up bras in crisp, striped cotton worn over puff-sleeved blouses and dangerously tight pencil skirts, pretty shirtwaisters with full skirts which opened to reveal tiny matching knickers, immaculately constructed wasp-waisted jackets in rough silk tweed, drape jersey dresses, an exquisite gold brocade evening coat with rose-pink lining, and an impossibly over-blown wedding dress in ivory silk, all of which may well have had the Dior clientele drooling. A typical Westwood twist came when the bride stumbled down the runway, blindfolded. Sex, it seems, is ever a concern – from corsets and heels so high that even the most agile of supermodels has problems walking in them, to the bondage trousers and rubber-wear of yesteryear. Nothing even remotely politically correct gets a look in at a Westwood show. Rather, provocation – and often blatant media manipulation – continues to be the name of the game.

On a more personal level, too, Westwood has her detractors. She is often accused of élitism, misogyny, extreme arrogance and worse. 'I've always said that clothes are about sex . . . Andreas's father is an ironsmith, he makes wrought iron, really wonderful things. He's going to make the staircase for our new shop in Conduit Street. He made a chastity belt for one of my collections once.

'We're like birds, you know. The peacocks don't mix with the hawks, the sparrows don't mix with the wrens . . . The question is not whether I'm being élitist. The question is whether being élitist is politically unsound.'

Certainly, she is given to highly reactionary, often not entirely well-thought-out generalisations. That said, she insists, 'I always vote against the worst. I vote Labour,' and stresses that her interest in tradition is purely academic and in no way conservative.

In the end, you can't help thinking that at least someone's got the nerve to express themselves against a culture that increasingly aligns itself with the middle class, liberal and bland. This is, after all, the Queen of Punk. Small wonder she objects to the Spice Girls and what she describes today as 'the horrible ethics of pushing your way through everything, just believing in yourself to the extent that you don't value anything other than your own egomaniacal ambition.

'I sound off about all sorts of things, but that doesn't mean that I'm not absolutely sincere. I know that my knowledge isn't great enough. I don't have enough reading inside me. Nobody does. But I say those things because nobody else is saying them.' Yet although she will no doubt continue to rail against what she personally considers to be unethical or unfair, the 56-year-old Westwood appears, for the moment at least, to be reasonably contented.

'I'm really lucky,' she says. 'It is a wonderful fortune to be able to tap into your potential. It's a glamorous job and I get a lot out of it.' Her husband in particular, both personally and professionally (they live and work together), makes life far more manageable than it used to be.

'The real mark of respect that I would pay Andreas is that I would be just as happy on my own,' she says. 'I mean, in most marriages, it's a compromise, but I don't really feel that I have to compromise too much, being with him. You know, I lived on my own for ten years, which means that I know I can, so I'm not jealous. I'm much older than him – I'm not saying how much older – but all I've ever wanted is for him to enjoy himself. If he didn't come home at night, I wouldn't care. I mean, sometimes he doesn't come home. I really don't mind. I'm not wanting anything from him. If he were to go away, which he won't . . . I've never been more secure about anybody in my life.'

Later, as I'm leaving her studio, she rushes after me.

'I don't want you to think I under-estimate Andreas,' she says. 'I want you to know that he is an exceptionally talented designer in his own right. I mean, I taught him and I've seldom met anyone so talented as he is. Before you go, I just wanted you to know that.'

With that, Vivienne Westwood, a vision in tomato red sheepskin slippers and followed by her dog, Alexandra, disappears up the stairs.

11
MANOLO BLAHNIK

HOW DOES IT FEEL TO BE FAMOUS?

DO YOU THINK I AM? I MEAN, MAYBE FOR THE FEW IN FASHION. MAYBE. I NEVER THINK ABOUT THAT. I MEAN, IF I DO TWO INTERVIEWS I FEEL OVER-EXPOSED.

Portrait: Nathalie Lamoral/Katz

Manolo Blahnik is standing at the top of a huge, flower-strewn marble staircase, the centrepiece of Paris's monolithic Opera Garnier. 'Look at me!' he shouts as I climb the stairs, a little intimidated by the grandeur of the surroundings and trying – but now failing – to keep a low profile. 'I'm with Nijinsky!'

I look up and, sure enough, he is standing – silver-haired and as immaculately groomed as ever in customary three-piece suit and Oxford brogues – alongside a pouting and posturing bare-torsoed figure, clad in nothing but a loincloth. Nijinsky it is then, and various other characters straight out of the Ballets Russes are prominently in attendance, too.

'Isn't it faaaaabulous!' cries Blahnik. 'I'm so haaaaappy!'

The occasion is the spring/summer haute couture show for the house of Christian Dior. Blahnik designed the shoes for the collection: he has been collaborating with John Galliano, couturier at the house, for many years now, crafting everything from strappy, spike-heeled sandals with jewel-coloured ribbons criss-crossing to mid-thigh, to Prince of Wales check, peep-toed sweet nothings, scattered with tiny but perfectly formed daisies.

'I love John!' Blahnik announces. 'He faxes me. He says: "Think Madame Casati [legendary Venetian socialite]", and that's that! I love him! So inspired! Such a privilege!'

For today's show, then, there are granny boots, only sky-high, fitted to mid-calf and crafted in the finest lace, and equally vertiginous satin mules, their stalactite heels covered in seed pearls. Blahnik fixed each one in place with his own fair hands in the first instance, to show the craftspeople involved in their making just how it might best be done. In this case the result is, quite simply, shoe heaven. Cinderella herself could not have dreamed of such exquisite footwear.

Back in London a few days later, their designer says that the shoes for this most recent collection were, in fact, more than a touch problematic. From a camel suede tote of his own design – a seemingly bottomless pit, large handbags being something of a signature – he pulls out a Latin American novel he's in the process of reading and, to illustrate his point, starts scribbling frenetically all over the inside of its battered front cover. His sketches are famous and every bit as lovely as the completed designs.

'This is more or less the shoes,' he says, holding the book up to me. (I wish he'd drawn them more or less over my book when I see them.) Then, going back to the drawing: 'Underneath her [he draws the sole of a shoe], it's got shiny metal, polished silver and gold, with nails in. Shiny, shiny. And when I see the location of the show, I say: "My God! Put tape on those things. Those girls are going to die coming down that marble staircase!" So they put tape [he draws again] like this and like that. Then they scrape [he draws some more] like this and like that. Otherwise, those poor girls, they would have killed themselves! Can you imagine!'

I can, I tell him, having myself fallen prey to more than a few near-death experiences teetering around in his shoes, negotiating grates in the pavement say, or – a disaster of unprecedented proportions – cobbles. As a child, I remember my mother and her girlfriends sticking their feet into his beautiful if precarious designs with double-sided sticky tape to avoid falling out of them. There can, however, be few more glamorous ways to come a cropper. If you've got to go, after all . . .

I am, of course, not alone in worshipping at the altar of the Manolo Blahnik shoe. Madonna once described his designs as 'wonderful – they last longer than sex'. Womenswear designer and general *grande fromage* socialite about (American) town, Carolina Herrara, who wears the shoes and uses them in her shows, has said, quite simply, that they gave her legs. Then there's Sandra Bernhard, who claims: 'His shoes are sexy and strappy as hell. The shoe itself looks like a woman.' And Isaac Mizrahi, typically flamboyant on Manolo Blahnik: 'He's Benjamin Franklin, Isaac Newton – a genius. I fall at his feet and worship at his temple.'

Blahnik has clad the famous feet of everyone from Tina Chow (he named a shoe after his great friend and helped her form the Aids Crisis Trust, one of the first Aids-related charities, back in 1987), Bianca Jagger ('So exotic, she's very serious now'), Jerry Hall and Diana Ross, to Kate Moss, Naomi Campbell and even Victoria Beckham, aka Posh Spice. 'Posh Spice,' Blahnik splutters incredulously. 'Really? I didn't know she wears them. Is that good? I'm not sure that's very good.'

The beautiful people of all generations can't get enough of Blahnik's shoes – referred to as 'Manolos' by those in the know. The word has become synonymous with the finest, most unashamedly feminine footwear in the world.

Manolo Blahnik speaks six different languages fluently and, often and quite confusingly, concurrently. This is made all the more bewildering by the fact that he thinks so fast that his tongue seems barely able to keep up with his brain. For this reason, his sentences are often endearingly scrambled. 'I was drawing stage sets and costumes for Midnight Summer's Dream,' he tells me. Or: 'Are you kidding? I love talking! I'm always talking off the top of my hairs!'

The son of a Czech father and Spanish mother (or, as he puts it, 'I have middle Europe in me'), he grew up in Santa Cruz de la Palma in the Canary Islands, where his family presided over a banana plantation.

'In the Canary Islands, you either had bananas or nothing!' he once proclaimed. 'There were no friends, no people, no cars, no TV on the island. You had to build yourself games.' Said games included tying his poor sister – and now business partner – Evangeline, to a post, then lighting a fire around her, inspired, apparently, by a Rhonda Flemming cowboy movie, as one is. Blahnik also whiled away the hours catching lizards – he fashioned little dresses for them, made out of sweet papers and the foil from cigarette packets, by all accounts.

Perhaps because he was prone to wreaking just this type of merry havoc, the Blahniks sent their son abroad to school, to the University of Geneva, where he studied law then literature. He decided he was not cut out for the legal profession when, legend has it, he passed out at the sight of a corpse in a class on forensic medicine. Then, on a break with some friends in France, Blahnik discovered Sixties Paris and fell in love with the place. He moved there in 1968, leaving his degree unfinished, and took a job at a typical swinging Sixties boutique called, rather aptly, Go. With itchy feet again by 1970 ('Good Lord! It was donkeys' years ago!'), he moved to London where he worked as PR and jeans buyer for Joan Burstein, then owner of designer emporium Feathers (she now owns Browns), before travelling to New York with a portfolio stuffed full of sketches of stage sets rather than shoes.

'You know,' he says today, 'I wanted to do films, to design the sets for films. But I didn't get on with the sort of people who do film. It's difficult for me to get on well with anybody because I'm too intimidated, or too neurotic. The film people, you know, there is such an element of fear between them, always this tremendous competition and insecurity, and that really gave me the blues.'

A happy change of career and, some might say, the discovery of his vocation in life was prompted by an appointment in New York with style guru Diana Vreeland. 'I had this huge portfolio, piles of drawings, very Mr Freedom, very naïve,' he explains. 'It had sets in, but also figures, people wearing the most horrendous things. At the time, I was mad about cherries. I had cherries winding round legs, right up to the thigh, hanging off handbags. Hideous beyond belief.' Vreeland clearly thought otherwise, so much so that, much later, Blahnik says, he even had the 'huge privilege' of designing footwear specially for her: 'Like little pumps, very flat, very long and paper-thin, because Mrs Vreeland was very frail by then.'

Back in Seventies London and fuelled by Vreeland's initial interest, Blahnik began designing shoes for Ossie Clark. 'The shoes were a bit wobbly, to tell you the truth. I didn't really understand about gravity very well and those girls in Ossie's shows, they were struggling for their lives.' Next came Fiorucci footwear. 'All those leopard shoes, they were mine. Everyone was wearing them. Nasty, ooooh. But it was very exciting.'

The proceeds helped to fund Zapata, a tiny shop hidden away just off the King's Road. It is as exclusive now as it was when it first opened, frequented by the rich and famous and any fashion frontrunner worth his or her salt. Now, however, Blahnik is also big business in America, where he has a much larger shop in New York, as well as concessions in more than a few chic department stores. His London shop, meanwhile, is today just called Manolo Blahnik, after its now famous owner.

Suggest to Manolo Blahnik that he might have made his mark, however, and he seems quite genuinely thrown –

distressed, even. 'Famous?' he wonders. 'Do you think I am? I mean, maybe for the few in fashion. Maybe. I never think about that. I never question that. I mean, if I do two interviews, I feel over-exposed.'

Despite an apparently voluble, if fragile nature, he is the soul of discretion where his clientele is concerned and spends most of his free time at his house in Bath, preferring the solitude and anonymity it affords him to a more sociable life in London. He lives alone, and has done for many years. He sleeps very little, watching films on video and reading into the small hours. That is, of course, when he's not in Italy, working at one of two small factories responsible for the production of his twice-yearly collections. He still makes all his own lasts.

He says of the people who produce his more elaborate designs: 'It is a tiny family. They have been doing those sorts of shoes for two hundred years so I am very lucky to have one of the last bastions of such wonderful hands.' No more than 80 pairs are made in a day, as compared to many tens of thousands for a more mainstream brand. No wonder, then, that they cost upwards of £200 a pair. Very few people who have ever been lucky enough to own a pair would say it wasn't well worth it. Blahnik's shoes do indeed give their wearers legs – legs long, thin and lovely, like a fashion illustration.

In the end, perhaps the most charming thing about this impeccably charming man is his insatiable appetite for his work. As well as designing his own line, he also has a loyal following of catwalk designers to make shoes for, including established names like Galliano, as well as relative newcomers Clements Ribeiro and Antonio Berardi. His sister, Evangeline, met Berardi, Blahnik says, while he was still at Central Saint Martins and he [Berardi] said: 'Do you think your brother would . . . ?' She said, 'Sure. Come and see him.'

There are some who might say that Blahnik was doing Berardi something of a favour – his mere presence in the front row of a fashion show is endorsement enough, let alone his actually designing the shoes. For his part, though, Blahnik says: 'I am blessed to have those young children. They keep me going, keep me excited. I am totally excited, more now than even when I started. I do one thing and I refine it and I love that.'

Although fashion commentators might wax lyrical about his designs ad infinitum, their creator seems never to be satisfied. 'I've done some good things, some valid, some not valid and some really horrible,' he says. 'But I keep them all, so I know what to avoid. I'm getting rid of things all the time. Out! Out! Out! Very soon, there will be nothing left to my shoes, just a band. I love almost non-existent things.'

Blahnik's shoes are already so delicate as to be barely there. Cut them back any further and rather than just being dangerous, they might well prove fatal. There are worse ways to go, however. Rest assured, Blahnik's following will be more than happy to carry on risking life and stick-thin limb in his shoes for many years to come.

12
TANYA
SARNE

HOW DID YOU END UP WORKING IN FASHION?

I DID IT BECAUSE I NEEDED TO PAY THE RENT… OH, AND
NOBODY ELSE WOULD EMPLOY ME.

Portrait: David Bailey

Tanya Sarne
Independent on Sunday Review magazine, 12 September 1999
Photography: Kent Baker. Styling: Sophia Neophitou
All clothes Ghost, autumn/winter 1999

'You have to keep moving. You have to, or you die.' Tanya Sarne, creator and sole owner of Ghost, takes a sip of red wine, a drag on a cigarette, then pauses to answer the office phone ('Well, someone's got to'). On a second line a friend is still waiting for her to finish giving the directions she has promised him, from a battered old A–Z which she is waving about in the other hand.

She continues in this way, as she has done for the last 20 minutes, despite the fact that we are over an hour late for our dinner reservation. Her stream of consciousness jumps from the trouble with the British fashion industry to the benefits of Britain pulling out of Europe, the redesign of the pool in her newly acquired LA home, the state of women's tennis, and the joys of shopping at Sainsbury's, Ladbroke Grove, at 4am on a Friday morning.

An inveterate workaholic, Sarne's train of thought inevitably returns to Ghost: the art direction of the next ad campaign, why a certain item of clothing has sold so much more than another, how to expand her business further without losing control.

When we arrive at our destination, a fish restaurant in Holland Park, Sarne swerves into a parking place which seems to emerge from nowhere for her, personally, just outside. The heroically patient owner of the restaurant greets us with air kisses and a bottle of champagne.

Such relentless, chaotic, very English eccentricity is, presumably, why so many observers assume that Sarne was the inspiration for Edina in *Absolutely Fabulous*; in fact the character is an amalgam of Sarne, her friend Lynne Franks and a handful of fashion's other more colourful characters. To reduce Sarne to such a cartoonish figure would be to under-estimate both her business acumen and her creative talent. Ghost's success is evidence that she knows exactly what she's doing. Everyone from Liam and Patsy to Kate and Naomi wears Ghost. In real rather than fashion life, too, women swear by the label, to keep cool on a summer's day in the office, or as the height of easy glamour at a black-tie dinner. And for those who can't afford the main line, Sarne has also been responsible for

three of Marks & Spencer's best-selling garments since the war: a pair of wide-legged elasticated trousers, a long, sleeveless dress and a bias-cut skirt.

With global domination in mind, next month sees the launch of the first Ghost fragrance, manufactured and distributed by Cosmopolitan Cosmetics, also responsible for Eau de Rochas and Gucci's Envy. Sarne now employs some 300 people and boasts a worldwide retail turnover of £30 million.

It was the break up of her marriage to Michael Sarne, director of the arthouse film Myra Breckenridge, that prompted Sarne to go into fashion. She married him in 1969, giving up her job as a teacher. In the early days of their partnership she spent her time hanging out with the glamorous likes of Jack Nicholson, Warren Beatty, Roman Polanski and Sharon Tate. Nine years later she found herself single again ('I was fed up with him sleeping with every starlet in town'), and with two young children to support.

Her reasons for entering fashion then were pragmatic rather than strictly vocational. 'I did it because I needed to pay the rent. I saw this gap in the market to create clothes for women with individuality . . . Oh, and nobody else would employ me.' She was also more aware of women's bodies than many designers, and more open to accommodating their needs. 'A woman's body is soft and rounded. Her weight fluctuates. She can lose or put on half a stone in a week. As a woman, I know how to cater to that.'

Sarne stumbled across a machine-washable viscose that looks like stiff grey net curtains to begin with but, when shrunk and dyed in muted colours, takes on the appearance of vintage crêpe. She made it up into designs to suit women of varying shape and size: skimpy petticoat dresses as well as more generous tunics; narrow trousers cropped at the ankle or wide-legged with their hems skimming the floor; tops with a halterneck, boat neck, v-neck, backless, sleeveless . . . It wasn't long before Ghost became an integral part of any fashionable wardrobe, gracing everyone from the very thin to the heavily pregnant alike.

More than 15 years later, aged 54, Sarne finds herself in

the happy position of having enough experience and financial stability to be able to develop her main line into a more fashion forward concern. Today, Ghost is shaking off its image as purveyor of easy, diaphanous dresses in favour of a more directional approach. The Ghost signatures remain, but the collection is more in line with current trends and more ambitious than it has been. Ghost fabrics now range from acrylic crêpe to georgette, tulle, silk, crisp cotton and knitwear, beaded and embroidered in ultra-feminine fashion with everything from lilies to dragonflies. For the past two seasons a Victorian theme has dominated in the form of high-necked button-through shirts and wasp-waisted, full, floor-sweeping skirts.

This hasn't been an entirely easy transition. 'Business has grown up in a higgledy-piggledy way around me,' says Sarne. 'I suppose that's very English. My main difficulty has always been the conflict between what actually sells and is commercial, and what is moving forward and directional. To keep that balance is really the ultimate skill. One has to have direction to be a fashion company, but there's a vest we've been doing for fifteen years that we still sell more of than we do anything else. It's always the mix. Without selling the really easy commercial pieces one couldn't have a business. But no one would be interested in the easy pieces if they hadn't been drawn to the label by the publicity attracted by the more directional pieces in the first place.'

This formula is, of course, not specific to Ghost. Calvin Klein, for example, makes rather more money out of the fragrances that carry his name than his clothes. Sarne is cautious not to over-state the importance of her own venture into the fragrance market, however.

'A perfume has to be enormously successful for the designer to make any money. It has to sell millions. And, you know, Ghost is known but we're not that well known. If the actual scent is fantastic, the bottle is beautiful and the packaging is good, there's no reason why it shouldn't be a very good product. But it's very difficult to do.'

The main purpose of a fragrance launch is to raise international awareness of a brand. There's a whole group of people who may not be able to afford Ghost's clothes, but who can and will buy the fragrance. Sarne says that the Ghost website, which has been up and running since April this year, selling more basic pieces, has received more than a million hits from people 'in places we've never heard of. The fragrance is just another way of reaching a broader audience.'

Sarne has converted the attic in her large West London home into a 'perfume room. I got hold of every perfume I possibly could. I had all these samples and I just stayed there night after night, sniffing away. It's an enormous pleasure. Very, very interesting.'

The end product, she says, will be 'very fresh, floral and on the sweet side. It's slightly old-fashioned but not; it develops into something very friendly . . . ' All of which is equally true of the clothes that have inspired its development.

What's kept Sarne going all these years? She is as passionate now as she was when she started and, although her tantrums are legendary, she is as likely to bite a young designer's head off as she is to offer them a bed for the night in her home, should they fall upon hard times.

'I'm responsible for feeding three hundred families from Skegness to York. I employ between sixty and seventy people full-time and have seven factories scattered across the UK that work exclusively for Ghost. There are people who have worked for me for seventeen years – since before this business even started – and they've given me their loyalty. There are a lot of days, especially when someone gives me their notice or something, when I wonder who I can give my resignation to.'

Not that Sarne would ever be likely to give up the label she started.

'I've always been into fashion. The challenge for me is fashion – being part of today, not yesterday. You can't stay still. You have to keep striving for something more, something better. That's what keeps me going. I like a difficult life.'

13
YOHJI YAMAMOTO

WHY DID YOU BASE YOUR COLLECTION ON THE BRIDE?

TO WEAR A WEDDING DRESS MEANS AT LEAST A KIND OF SUCCESS. THE UNIFICATION AND COMBINATION OF MEN AND WOMEN. THIS IS WHAT IS CALLED HAPPINESS…

Portrait: Kazumi Kurigami

Yohji Yamamoto
Independent on Sunday Review magazine, 24 January 1999
Photography: Jane McLeish. Styling: Sophia Neophitou
All clothes Yohji Yamamoto, spring/summer 1999

Interviewing Yohji Yamamoto is nothing if not a challenge. To resort to the 'inscrutable' stereotype seems predictable if not actually insulting, but where this particular designer is concerned, it is only a matter of time. Ask him to describe his spring/summer collection, for example.

'Like a pendulum,' he muses. 'Real clothes and costume, yesterday and today. With my two hands, I have mixed the ridiculousness and absurdity of costume and the boringness of real clothes, like creating the salad dressing for nouvelle cuisine.'

Next, try gauging exactly why he chose to base his show from start to finish on the bride and the widow. 'To wear a wedding dress means at least a kind of success,' says Yamamoto. 'The unification and combination of men and women. This is what is called happiness, in terms of the symbolism of the ritual of the human body.'

As for the widow part of the equation: 'You wouldn't become a widow if you didn't marry,' declares Yamamoto. True, though hardly revealing. But then fashion has come to expect this kind of statement from such an enigmatic and determinedly aloof designer.

Mention the name Yohji Yamamoto to anyone even remotely interested in fashion and you are likely to provoke an unprecedented response. Yohji, they will say, is far more than a fashion designer, he is a poet. Yohji doesn't just make dresses, he creates works of art. Add to this the fact that Yamamoto is given to performing impromptu live guitar performances to suitably bewildered audiences in downbeat Tokyo bars, and you begin to get the picture. Among his other accolades, Yohji Yamamoto is the Leonard Cohen of fashion.

In the face of adversity, however, the world keeps trying to unravel the mystery that is Yamamoto. In 1989 director Wim Wenders spent 80 minutes attempting to do just this in his seminal documentary about the designer, 'Notebook On Cities And Clothes'. 'What secret has he discovered this Yamamoto?' the star-struck director wonders. 'What does he know about me? About everybody?' Suffice it to say, by the end, Wenders – and indeed his audience – is none the wiser.

Yohji Yamamoto was born in Tokyo in 1943. His mother was a seamstress, his father was drafted and killed in the Second World War. 'He went against his will,' says Yohji, in 'Notebook'. 'When I think of my father I realise that the war is still raging inside me.'

After completing a law degree at Keio University, Yamamoto Junior switched to fashion, working with his mother until he set up as a designer in his own right in the late Sixties. In the early Eighties, Yamamoto emerged on the international fashion circuit – one of the first ever overseas-based designers invited to show in Paris. Up to this point, no one in this chintz- and taffeta-filled world knew anything much about contemporary Japanese fashion. Black wasn't even a colour.

Yamamoto's first show changed all that forever. A dour army of grim-faced models, their hair shorn, their faces painted white, marched down the catwalk to the thud of an amplified electronic heartbeat. Their clothes – huge, dark, asymmetric shapes, in distressed fabrics or peppered with holes – were a million miles away from anything the audience, comprising the world's most fêted fashion commentators, had ever dreamed of. To make matters more difficult still, the models' shoes were flat (no one did flat shoes), rustic even. The fashion fraternity, almost in its entirety, was lost for words, so much so that architectural critics were turned to for points of reference.

And it was architects – along with artists, writers and anyone who was anyone in creative circles – who wore Yohji. His clothes were deemed too 'challenging', and certainly not glamorous or flattering enough for fashion editors and models. Almost 20 years on, people still talk about Yamamoto as if he were some sort of mystic – a true artist, unlike any other fashion designer.

His continued reluctance to expound on his work aside, Yohji Yamamoto, now accepted by the fashion establishment, is almost unanimously revered as one of the greats. It is not uncommon these days for his audience (admittedly one prone to extreme bouts of over-emotion) to be moved to tears by the sheer beauty of it all.

What's more, Yamamoto, just like other designers, now produces more affordable clothing lines, accessories and

even a fragrance, although in the case of the latter in particular the designer gives the impression of having been bullied into it by rather more mundane and financially motivated parties.

When I interviewed Yamamoto around the time 'Yohji' the fragrance launched, I enquired whether he had been inspired by any other great perfumes. Yamamoto appeared – quite alarmingly – almost to wince in pain.

'I don't really like perfume,' he answered, abruptly. This wouldn't have mattered if I hadn't been instructed by over-anxious press officers to concentrate on that rather than the clothes. Worse still, an army of executives in suits, the brains behind the fragrance, were also in attendance, waiting eagerly for the great designer to pour forth on the merits of the precious elixir – an utterly futile expectation, as it turned out.

Yamamoto's unwillingness to market himself is not the only thing that sets him apart from his contemporaries. To say he is aesthetically sensitive would be an under-statement. Take his reaction to high heels or heavy make-up as example.

'Where I was born,' Yamamoto once told me, speaking so quietly that I had to strain to hear him, 'there were very many prostitutes. And they were wearing high heels and strong lipstick. And really, I was afraid. I was scared. Because they looked very, very wild. Very, very wild and scary. Not natural. And after I became a designer, I still have the same reaction to high heels and strong lipstick. I get very scared.'

These days, though, despite any underlying fears, whatever Yamamoto touches leads to hyperbole, extreme even by fashion standards. Jewel-coloured floral devore evening dresses – sent out two years ago – were pretty and feminine but still resolutely modern; attaching Belle Epoque-inspired gowns to the body by knotted coils of silk was nothing short of technical genius. Last season, Yamamoto took onlookers' breath away when he sent out Jodie Kidd in a wedding dress so over-blown that it threatened to take the three front rows with it as she swept down the catwalk. Needless to say, we would all have gone

quite willingly. In fact, the dress was so well received that, this season, Yamamoto chose to expand upon the very same theme.

To the dulcet tones of the 'Wedding March' – straining from what sounded like an unusually dilapidated piano – one model after another emerged in the type of unashamedly romantic gown that, at first sight, wouldn't look out of place in a lavish costume drama. The designer is fascinated, he explains, by the fact that even the most modern and minimally dressed woman can't help but resort to fantasy and, more significantly, tradition when it comes to her own wedding. Yamamoto is catering to the dreams of the most contemporary brides.

There were fluid white trouser suits (the widow's version in inky black), floor-sweeping skirts which, when removed, revealed slim, knee-length versions worn underneath (just in case our heroine finds herself running for a bus, say). The most dramatic wedding dress of all had zips sewn into it which, when opened, disclosed a pair of ivory pumps, a fashionably crushed *My Fair Lady* picture hat and a calico bouquet – is it a dress or a suitcase, you might not unfairly ask? Yamamoto's juxtaposition of the traditional and the modern had never before seemed so accomplished. It was the show of the Paris season.

I ask the designer – who one might assume was rather less than conventional – whether he approves of the institution of marriage. 'The old meaning lies in the conventional unwritten rules which relieve people around you. The new meaning is to submit and announce to the person in charge of the family register that a man and woman will be together and acquire the nation's approval and permission.'

Yes, yes, but do you approve of marriage as an institution, Mr Yamamoto? 'Can you approve of this? I'm an Asian and was brought up through the culture of Christianity, so I may be misinterpreted or misunderstood.'

Misinterpreted and misunderstood, perhaps, although one would hope not as often as he used to be. For while Yamamoto's words may continue to perplex, his clothes speak volumes.

14 TOM FORD

HOW WOULD YOU DEFINE SEX APPEAL?

SEX APPEAL TO ME IS SOMEONE WHO'S RELAXED. I DON'T THINK YOU CAN BE SEXY IF YOU'RE NOT RELAXED. ESPECIALLY IN AMERICA, THE BEAUTY STANDARD HAS BECOME SO UPTIGHT, SO WORKED. I DON'T FIND THAT SEXY AT ALL. SEXY PEOPLE ARE USUALLY VERY COMFORTABLE WITH THEMSELVES – COMFORTABLE WITH THEMSELVES WHILE YOU'RE FALLING APART.

The Independent magazine, 16 January 1999
Photography: Julie Sleaford. Styling: Sophia Neophitou
All clothes Gucci, spring/summer 1999

In appearance at least, Tom Ford more than lives up to his reputation as fashion's modern-day matinee idol. He arrives at Blakes Hotel very slightly tanned, more than slightly toned, perfectly groomed with a dense crop of thick, dark hair and suitably impressive designer stubble, and immaculately, but immaculately dressed.

'I'm so sorry I'm late,' he sighs in an unbelievably sexy, all-American drawl. 'To be honest, I'm just so tired I dropped off on the sofa before I came out. And now look at me.' He looks down at himself in dismay. 'I'm a mess – completely covered in dog hair.'

He is, I tell him, no more covered in dog hair than I am, which is, in fact, not very covered in dog hair at all because, unlike Tom Ford, I don't actually own a dog.

Instead, the designer is, on this occasion as always, clad from head-to-toe in his own entirely dog-hair-free designs.

'Of course!' he exclaims, as if it were the most obvious thing in the world. 'Gucci jeans' – they're dense black, turned up just so, to reveal that tell-tale famous red and green Gucci stripe running alongside the inside seam – 'Gucci boots, Gucci shirt, Gucci jacket . . . ' He pauses for a moment before adding triumphantly: 'Gucci everything.'

Like any modern-day matinee idol worth his salt, even before he has had the chance to sit down Ford is subjected to the full star treatment – mobbed! – by a perhaps inappropriately excitable member of staff. This is Blakes, after all, London base to everyone from Dolce & Gabbana to Madonna. Anyone who works at the hotel is exposed to more than their fair share of serious glamour. This woman's response is therefore unprecedented. But then matinee idols are admittedly rather thin on the ground these days.

'Oh, Mr Ford. I just had to introduce myself to you,' she gushes – she can't help herself, clearly. 'We just love your stuff here.' She's clasping Ford's perfectly manicured hand so ferociously, it seems she may never relinquish it. Ever the perfect gentleman, Ford would rather die than show it but he is clearly in some pain – if not actually physical then psychological at least. 'We have your watches. You know, Gucci watches. We just love them, love what you do.'

It is by now the stuff of fashion legend that, in less than five years, Tom Ford has singlehandedly transformed Gucci, a tired old status label and family concern beleaguered by in-fighting and intrigue, to the label to see and be seen in. Only four years ago, Gucci was facing bankruptcy, worth a meagre – by international fashion standards – $250,000. At the time of writing, Gucci boasts a worldwide retail volume of $2.2 billion.

Today, Gucci is the label of choice of just about any fashion editor, model or general jetsetter about town. Anyone who was anyone just had to have Ford's boot-cut pants one season; his long, slinky Halston-inspired dresses the next. Gwyneth Paltrow, Uma Thurman and Meg Mathews are all Gucci devotees. Madonna wore jewel-encrusted Gucci jeans and skinny leather jacket for her recent TV interview with Johnny Vaughan. In *Spice Girls The Movie* there's even a Gucci joke: 'What shall I wear? The little Gucci dress, the little Gucci dress, or the little Gucci

dress.' The Great British high street, meanwhile, is today jam-packed with Gucci copies, in store before the originals that inspire them have even made the rails.

Ford has had quite an effect on the designer fashion industry, too. Gucci was the first established fashion house to employ the services of a bright young American or European designer to preside over this round of image overhauls. Since Ford took the helm and, in his able hands, the label became an overnight, spectacular success, other more established companies have been quick to follow suit. Galliano has taken over at Christian Dior, Alexander McQueen at Givenchy, Marc Jacobs at Louis Vuitton, and Michael Kors at Celine.

It is just as it should be that Ford's own appearance is every bit as seductive as the advertising campaigns which promote his label. Originally photographed by superstar fashion photographer Mario Testino, these showed the kind of utterly gorgeous young men and women, draped here, there and everywhere, that make us lesser mortals feel somehow outdated, shabby even, as though we really ought to invest in the label – or at least buy the fragrance – if we are to have any life at all. Significantly, and perhaps Gucci's finest endorsement of all, Ford, sitting today on an over-stuffed banquette beside me, positively exudes fragrant wafts of his self-styled and very aptly entitled perfume, Envy. It is true that we could all be forgiven for wanting to be him.

'Sex appeal to me,' Ford purrs, sexily enough, 'is someone who's relaxed. I don't think you can be sexy if you're not relaxed. Especially in America, the beauty standard has become so uptight, so worked. I don't find that sexy at all. You know, sexy people are usually very comfortable with themselves – comfortable with themselves while you're falling apart.'

The Gucci look then is louche, lean, a little flashy, if always intended to be ironically so, and at the same time, and very cleverly, ever so slightly déshabillé: a cobweb-knit sweater pulled deliberately off one shoulder; a pair of trousers that sits dangerously low, grazing the hip bones.

There's only a hint now of the pre-Ford ludicrously ostentatious branding – the word Gucci carved oh-so-discreetly on the bone buttons of a slouchy pair of trousers; tiny interlocking Gs gracing the perfect kitten heel or the glossy black lining of a narrowly tailored jacket. Wearing it might look easy – Ford himself makes it seem entirely effortless – but every last detail has been pored over by the designer himself. Attempt to buy a Gucci belt, for example, and you'll find that the current model has only three holes – any more would just look a mess – and is specifically designed to be fastened through the middle hole. Lose any weight and you'll ruin the symmetry; gain any and, frankly, liposuction's your only option – and arguably cheaper than forking out on a new belt.

'I think people should look after themselves,' Ford says, very firmly. 'Plastic surgery? Sure? Why not? But there's plastic surgery and plastic surgery. There's plastic surgery that leaves you so tightly pulled you don't look like a

human being any more. I think people become obsessive about it. But if, you know, you have a saggy chin or something you need to have fixed and if it's done properly . . . Of course, I'm big on being thin. That doesn't mean you have to be skin and bone but you absolutely should be as fit as you can be.'

It might seem like an unforgiving formula but it's also one that has worked. More than any other designer, Tom Ford will go down in history as the man responsible for dressing the final years of the 20th century, just as Courreges, say, dressed the Sixties, Saint Laurent the Seventies, and Armani the Eighties. The knowingly super-slick, super-sexy, hard-edged glamour that the Gucci label has come to signify is perfect end-of-the-millennium fodder. Small wonder then that the *New York Times* recently described Ford as 'the ultimate *fin de siècle* designer'.

A self-confessed control freak, Ford is now responsible for no less than 11 merchandise lines, from handbags and watches to cat and dog collars and soft furnishings. He is also busy personally controlling the revamping of Gucci stores worldwide as we speak – right down to the sinks in the guest bathrooms (guest bathrooms!) of the recently refurbished London store. Ford is, by all accounts, very proud of these sinks, of the fact that the water runs down the edges of the basin rather than the centre before making its way down the (Gucci) plug hole. But then, with Gucci, you don't just wear the clothes, you live the lifestyle. Ford himself has a Gucci fur blanket on his bed in his Paris home and, not to be outdone, his dog, a terrier called John (a regular name for an above averagely lucky mutt), is the proud owner of a leather Gucci dog bed.

Ford, 37, was born and raised in Texas. Fashion folklore has it that at age 12 he owned his first pair of Gucci shoes.

'It's true,' he admits. 'People used to tease me. But, you know, wearing anything Gucci in Texas was just totally about status. After all, the people who settled in Texas came from nowhere, they started off as farmers or ranchers so it's a flashier society than you'd find here.'

His parents were both real-estate agents. His mother, who Ford has said looked just like Tippi Hedren – all pinned-up ice-blonde hair, tailored clothes and high heels – and his paternal grandmother both influence his aesthetic.

'My grandmother was – still is, she's eighty-seven now – this big, loud Texan woman. You know, she had six husbands. Very attractive, very beautiful. She wore Courreges lace pantsuits in the Sixties and had turquoise bracelets right up her arms. She was a big influence on me as a kid because she was a cartoon. You could see her one time and she was one way and the next she looked completely different . . . ' He pauses then adds as an afterthought: 'You know, she always jingled and clinked when she moved.'

The designer went on to spend his teenage years in Sante Fe, then moved to New York to go to college. When a classmate invited him to Studio 54, then at its most heavily fashionable, he knew he'd arrived. It was there, he claims today, that he first discovered he was gay, and it

wasn't long before he was a regular fixture at the club as well as, of course, at Andy Warhol's Factory. 'I'm not sure he wasn't a bit evil,' Ford has said about Warhol. 'But he was so smart.'

Neglecting his college studies almost entirely, handsome Tom Ford set to acting in TV commercials – at one point there were 12 running simultaneously – to keep him in the manner to which he was accustomed. Eventually, he ended up at Parsons School of Art in Manhattan, studying not fashion but architecture.

'I was living in Paris and in my third year of Parsons and, honestly, I just woke up one morning and thought, what am I doing? Architecture was just way too . . . It was just so serious. Oh my God, the pretentiousness of architecture! So I realised I was getting more excited every month buying *Vogue* and I thought, you know, this is what I love, this is what I seem to be drawn to the whole time. I mean, every architectural project I ever did, I worked a dress into it somehow. So I realised that fashion was the right balance between art and commerce and that was it.'

There followed a period assisting New York-based designer Cathy Hardwick, then, later, Perry Ellis. That was until September 1990, when, with Dawn Mello, former president of the chic New York department store Bergdorf Goodman, installed as creative director at Gucci, Tom Ford moved to Milan to design an expanded womenswear line for the label.

Ford still attributes his interest in the commercial side of the business to the fact that he cut his fashion teeth on New York's Seventh Avenue. Certainly, he's a far cry from the tortured artist agonising over the crafting of whimsical garments. 'I love talking about money,' he says. 'And I love thinking of how to make more of it! I don't understand people who say that business and creativity aren't compatible. You know, I started out in New York and, really, if the collection you designed didn't sell, you were fired the next day. What some fashion designers do is art and I have an incredible respect for it, but I don't pretend to be anything other than a commercial designer and I'm proud of that.'

It is equally, he says, his sense of commerce that inspires him to look at the label as a whole rather than simply occupying himself with the business of designing clothes.

'I enjoy it all,' he says, 'the advertising campaigns, the store designs, the packaging, working on all these different product packages, working out strategy and where to go next with it. That's what fascinates me.'

Ford's breakthrough collection for Gucci came in March 1995, almost five years after he started working for the company. When a blonde and tousled Kate Moss came down Ford's runway in the most perfectly cut blue velvet trousers known to man, even though they did appear to be flared, teamed with a skinny shirt that plunged right down to the navel, the fashion world couldn't believe its eyes. The collection was basically inspired by the Seventies but, unlike any other Seventies revival that had come before it, Ford's was far more than mere pastiche. This was the

Seventies brought right up to date with a bang. It was also the most blatantly sexy thing that had been seen at the international collections for seasons. For the first time in years, Gucci made the front pages of fashion glossies and newspapers. Tom Ford had arrived.

But could he live up to the hype? He certainly did so with his next collection, and with fluid black and white evening dresses finished with lozenges of gleaming metal, in particular. Once again, these were the most photographed clothes of the season.

Then, having reinvented the Seventies and made them hip again, Ford moved on to the Eighties: killer metal heels, shoulder-pads and even sack dresses. This was not as easy on the eye as the collections that came before it, and some said an Eighties revival before the Nineties had even come to a close was taking the retro thing a little too far. But what Ford says, goes. Cue the barrage of Eighties revival stories that filled the fashion pages that same season.

By March last year, however, there was the feeling that Ford had taken his impeccably edited and even more impeccably finished brand of glamour as far as it could go; that the excitement that had sprung up around the label was something that even he would no long be able to sustain. What's more, the reviews for his two most recent collections were far from unanimously positive. This could simply be seen as the nature of the fashion industry, however – to be everyone's darling one minute, only to be cast aside the next.

'Of course negative reviews upset me,' Ford says now. 'When you work hard at something, you want it to be successful. You know, I went through a period, about a year ago, that was tough because I'd worked to get to a certain point and I was there. I had everything I wanted. Even on a personal level. I live with someone I love. I've been with him for twelve years. I have a wonderful family, lots of friends, plenty of money, success, everything.

'So I thought to myself: Is this it? And, you know, sometimes you have to find a new goal and perhaps that goal isn't material, perhaps it's a personal thing. And during that period, yes, there were times when I didn't know whether I could do design any more. Oddly enough, if you look at the collections from that period, they seem to me now to be a little, well, sad, really.'

It couldn't have helped that the economic crisis in Asia last year saw Gucci stock plummet (almost half of the company's sales are in Asia), or, for that matter, that last summer arch rival Prada spent $240 million buying up 9.5 per cent of Gucci's equity. Ford refuses to comment. His spring/summer collection, however, is more than ample evidence of how this designer functions in the face of adversity. Not to be beaten, like any high achiever worth mentioning, Tom Ford took a big – if, as always, cleverly calculated – risk.

As the first outfit came out on the runway in Milan last October, it was clear that Gucci was set to undergo something of a transformation. Gone was the worldly, intimidating, thoroughly metropolitan glamour of past collections in favour of a far more optimistic and eclectic aesthetic, a more fresh-faced and, on the face of it, naïve approach. Ford put aside his monochromatic palette, too, a tall order for a man who, until recently, filled his entire closet with black. For spring/summer 1999, Gucci had exploded into colour.

There were psychedelic print dresses with little frills round the neckline, faded ripped-up jeans dripping with diamanté and, it seemed, anything else Ford could lay his hands on and finished with feather patch pockets. Surrounded, as fashion editors have been for too long, by wannabe conceptual fashion and a veritable ocean of grey, Gucci's latest collection, at long last, was what the industry had been waiting for. And Ford – and herein lies perhaps his greatest talent – had handed it over before anyone had even realised that that was what was needed. He received a standing ovation and is the man of the moment once more.

'It started out with the fact that I wanted the collection to be optimistic,' he says. 'And colourful. And a little bit over the top. I wanted it to be fun. Some of the inspiration is from Las Vegas and Liberace. You know, Vegas fascinates me because you have this place with no history and you have people who come to it with no background, no money, nothing, and then they might become rich. So they don't fall back on what they've been taught is beautiful or acceptable, they create their own beauty. And sometimes the vile, vulgar things, or the things we perceive as tasteless in our society, are actually really beautiful. Like diamonds. Culturally, a lot of us have been taught that overdoing diamonds is tacky, but, you know, they're beautiful, they sparkle and shine. If you can have them all over, then why not?'

Why not, indeed? Although there's rather more to the collection than that. Beaded belts, shoes and bags have their roots in native America; references to Ford's native Texas and Santa Fe are much in evidence, as are more to Swinging London – the original, not the Nineties rehash. Perhaps most importantly of all, though, Ford's spring/summer collection is a tribute to his grandmother.

'You know, it's funny. I thought it was completely eclectic but my mother watched the tape of the show and she said, "It's just totally your grandmother." I think a lot of our beauty ideals must be formed when we're kids.'

So, this summer season Tom Ford looks set to find his way back onto the front covers, back at the very top of Fashion's Most Wanted lists. With his drive and determination, it seems churlish not to conclude that he deserves his reputation and all the fame and wealth that goes with it.

Ford is currently setting up home in London: at the moment he moves almost constantly between Florence, Paris, Milan and America. Unsurprisingly, then, he is looking to stay put for some if not all of his time.

There's only one thing about this particular capital city that irks him, however. 'It's your damn quarantine laws,' he snipes. Surely, I wonder, his dog doesn't travel with him.

'Oh, but he does,' Ford insists. 'He has his own frequent-flyer card – Air France'. The epitome of glamour.

15
DONATELLA VERSACE

WHAT WOULD YOU SAY MOTIVATES YOU?

I LOVE MUSIC. IT'S THE MOST IMPORTANT CULTURE OF TODAY. MOVIES AND MUSIC, THOSE ARE THE CULTURES OF THIS AGE, WHAT YOUNG PEOPLE LISTEN TO OR GO TO SEE. YOU HAVE TO BE RECEPTIVE TO EVERYTHING THAT'S NEW – IT IS THE FUTURE. I'M ALWAYS DRIVEN TO PUSH FORWARD. SEARCHING FOR WHAT IS MODERN – THAT IS WHAT MOTIVATES ME.

Portrait: Harry Borden/Katz

Donatella Versace
The Guardian Weekend magazine, 18 April 1998
Photography: Donald Christie. Styling: Karl Plewka
All clothes Atelier Versace, Gianni Versace, Versus, spring/summer 1998

There'll come a time when Donatella Versace's name will appear without her brother Gianni's alongside it. But for now – and probably for some time to come – as far as most of the world is concerned, she is still the sister, the successor, the heir. When Gianni Versace was shot dead in South Beach, Miami, last summer, Donatella inherited the creative legacy of a fashion empire worth an estimated $800 million. It is, along with Giorgio Armani, probably the most famous designer label in the world. As well as the responsibility for maintaining the Versace name, 40-year-old Donatella inherited all the power and glamour that goes with it, the spotlight of her brother's celebrity, the fame. She already had the fortune: along with her older brother, Santo, the company's far less visible chief executive, Donatella owns half the Versace estate, while Gianni bequeathed his 50 per cent to her daughter, Allegra.

Donatella's New York residence – a $7 million townhouse on the ultra-stylish Upper East Side, a fashionable stone's throw from Central Park – was once the house her brother lived in. From the outside the place seems surprisingly under-stated, if coolly grand. Were it not for the bronze Medusa head (the Versace signature) that takes pride of place on the front door, you could easily not notice it. There are no obvious signs of security – no doorman, no video entry-phone, no security cameras; just a doorbell, the old-fashioned kind – a reminder of Donatella's observation that her brother Gianni 'had no idea how famous he was'.

It's 85 degrees outside but, inside, the Versace residence is as dimly lit and cool as a Florentine church. The heady aroma of lilies and the perfumed candles dotted all around fills the air. In a private courtyard outside there's a fountain and a pond strewn with the petals of pink roses, Donatella's favourite flower. Inside, in one corner of the hall there is a spiral staircase, carpeted in leopard print, and a mosaic marble floor. Black marble columns flank the entrance into the main reception room, where there are more Picassos on display than there are at the Tate. Gianni was a passionate collector.

Today, however, Donatella has less cerebral things than art on her mind. She's downstairs in the kitchen, by all accounts swapping recipes with a member of staff. While I wait for her I am offered iced water from a crystal decanter and a silver platter of small but perfectly formed sandwiches, painstakingly cut into circles the size of pound coins.

When the lady of the house finally appears, her diminutive frame seems dwarfed by the grandeur of her surroundings. She's dressed in black, as she has been since her brother's murder – black T-shirt, black jeans and shiny black, spike-heeled boots. She hates her legs: she always wears high heels, she says, laughing, because 'they're way too short'.

In person, her features are far softer than they appear in photographs, as is her manner. Her media incarnation as super-charged bimbo meets post-punk Barbie doll seems as wildly exaggerated as the charges of vulgarity still brought against the Versace label. After all, in Italy –

particularly throughout the Eighties, when she came to the public's attention – people dress like Donatella Versace. It is part of the culture.

She curls up beside me in the corner of an over-stuffed sofa and lights up a Marlboro – full strength. The lady doesn't do Lights. She's got a filthy cold, she tells me, running her fingers through her trademark platinum-blonde tresses. Her voice sounds all the more husky, rich like treacle, for it. She's exhausted – but she looks like the proverbial million dollars. And this despite the fact that it is only two days after the autumn/winter '98 showing of the Versus line – her first show in New York since her brother's death – and less than a month after the Milan collections, where she presented Gianni Versace main line.

All eyes in the American fashion capital are, at this moment, on Donatella Versace. Gianni handed over the Versus label to his sister more than five years ago.

'It's my baby,' she purrs. 'It's the first thing Gianni gave me. He put me in charge, completely in charge. So I felt so honoured. But I was also scared that Gianni wasn't going to like what I was doing.'

Although I had been warned to be sensitive in alluding to Gianni, as it is only eight months since he died and Donatella is still grieving, her conversation is littered with such easy references to her brother. She ploughs ahead in English, although she is by no means fluent, seeming anxious to express herself as fully as possible. For such a big-name designer, the subject of so many rumours, she is unusually open, the result, perhaps, of having been thrust into a glaring spotlight overnight. Small wonder, then, that her entourage is fiercely protective of her. Like a lot of Italians, she quite obviously loves to talk, and yet interviews with Donatella are hard come by.

The latest Versus show – at Roseland, the famous New York music venue – was a typically star-studded affair: Versace-clad Liz Hurley and Hugh Grant, Whitney Houston and Bobby Brown, Woody Allen and Soon Yi, Minnie Driver, Lenny Kravitz, Sheryl Crow, Dennis Hopper and Rupert Everett all took pride of place in the front row. Like her brother before her, Donatella knows how to attract the glitterati – and how to dress them – and she knows how to give great party. A live thrash-metal soundtrack came courtesy of the Foo Fighters, who played on the catwalk as the models came down. The clothes themselves were equally the typical mix of Versace-esque glamour and the harder, urban, rock-chick edge that characterises Donatella's own label – and Donatella herself, for that matter. She is, in many ways, the ultimate rock chick.

'I love music,' she says. 'It's the most important culture of today. Movies and music, those are the cultures of this age, what young people listen to or go to see.' It could be her brother talking. 'You have to be receptive to everything that's new – it is the future. I'm always driven to push forward. Searching for what is modern – that is what motivates me.'

It is this love of young people, and her insatiable appetite for the new, that made her indispensable to Gianni. 'I'm open to everything,' she says. 'All the new people I have employed are young.' Four of them are recent graduates from London's Central Saint Martins.

'They don't have too much experience, and that's the best thing, because of the amount of passion they put into their work. They are in a dream, the people from Saint Martins! I brought them to the archives, you know, the Versace archives, to show them the sort of clothes Gianni has done, and they were, like, "Wow!" '

Her passion for modernity is equally relentless. She constantly refers to things as being 'demode'. 'To design clothes with an ideal woman in mind is demode. Women today are so different, interesting, intelligent, with a lot of attitude. I think individuality is what inspires me. I would like all women to be able to wear my clothes, but women with attitude, especially. They know what they're doing. They believe in what they are doing. They're very conscious of who they are.' To wear clothes that are too 'cluttered' is demode, too. 'You can't go around with too much decoration. It's not a society that permits this any more. I mean, yes, you go out in the night and you wear a fabulous dress, that's okay. But day clothes . . . they have to be fun, they have to have style, but they have to be wearable, too . . . I think everything is so demode,' she says excitedly, then, quite sweetly, 'Myself, too. Maybe I'm demode! Hahahaha.'

Just in case, she deliberately employs people who have very different ideas from her own. 'It's important to have that contrast,' she says. 'They like certain things, in one direction. I like certain others. I think that's interesting.'

While Gianni was alive, Donatella operated as the world's most glamorous scout – hanging out with the up-and-coming beautiful people, staying up all night in clubs, throwing parties for the likes of Madonna and Elton John. 'I love to sleep,' she tells me, 'but I don't sleep so much. It makes me think I'm missing something. It's a problem for me, sleeping.'

What's more, Gianni listened to his sister – there were very few other people around him who would have dared criticise his work. Because of Donatella, it is widely acknowledged, the Versace label, unlike others of its era, has kept up with the times. Until recently, Donatella was continually described as Gianni's muse. 'This is not very amusing,' is her sharply dismissive retort. She knows, of course, that, both professionally and personally, she meant much more to her brother than that.

Since her childhood, her brother Gianni's influence over her has been all-pervasive. Even her preternaturally blonde hair is yet another of his legacies. 'I was eleven,' she says. 'Gianni brought to the house a friend of his who was a hairdresser. We had to hide him from my mother.' Sadly, she says, the hairdresser's work was so discreet that it was, in the end, barely there. 'He put in a few highlights, but nobody noticed,' laments Donatella, whose predilection for a less-than-demure appearance was, even at that tender age, clearly in evidence. She was never one to do things by half. 'I was furious. I thought, "What's going on here?" He said, "No, I don't want to do too much, I want it to be subtle." But I wanted him to do it properly. So I kept adding to it, and adding to it . . . '

As she talks she gesticulates extravagantly, like any self-respecting Italian. On one finger she famously wears a huge yellow diamond – her most prized possession, a gift from Gianni. 'Actually,' she says, 'Gianni was looking all over the world for a pink diamond for me, because he knew I loved them. He was so sweet. He knew I loved jewellery. He loved jewellery, too. He couldn't wear it, so I wore it.'

Donatella and Gianni Versace were born in Reggio di Calabria, southern Italy. Their mother, Francesca, was a dressmaker – she died when Donatella was 20. Their father, Antonio, was, by all accounts, a rather remote figure. Although Santo was the eldest Versace child, and grew up alongside them, the significant relationship was always the one between Gianni and Donatella, who were inseparable. Gianni once said: 'I think if I were to marry, I would look for a girl like Donatella. Our friendship was from when we were children. We were always together. I can be in China or on the moon, we'll still speak a hundred times a day.'

In the late Seventies, when Gianni was making a name for himself in Milan, Donatella studied literature at university in Florence. 'My mother didn't want me to be in fashion,' she says, mischievously. 'She was in the fashion business, so was my brother, and she thought it was too crazy for me, the whole thing, that the fashion business was too crazy for a girl. She wanted me to be married with children, to be independent, yes, but not to do a crazy life. She tried to protect me a bit.'

Strong-willed from the start, however, Donatella knew that she didn't need protecting. She studied during the week, then travelled to Milan at the weekend to help out in her brother's studio. This was, at the time, nothing more than a couple of rooms in an apartment with two assistants who still work for the company to this day. In 1979, when Donatella was already designing accessories for the Versace label, Gianni and Donatella met the man she would later marry, the American model Paul Beck. The three became so close that, predictably, rumours persisted that he was Gianni's lover before he married Donatella in 1983. When Beck himself was asked about this he shrugged it off. 'I think that's what it seemed like, on the surface, because we were always together,' he told *Vanity Fair*. 'We were always at shows and dinners together in New York, so I think there was a lot of talk. I would say, if anybody, Gianni's my best friend. Yeah, I've never denied being a very good friend of Gianni's, but it's never been more than that.' Beck now produces the Versace advertising campaigns.

It was, of course, during the Eighties that the Versace label rose to worldwide prominence. The heady mix of black leather and metal mesh, the blinding colour and skintight fit of Gianni Versace's clothes encapsulated that era perfectly. Donatella wore the clothes and lived the life to the full. The enduring image of the label's allure is that, not long after the release of George Michael's 'Freedom' at the autumn/winter 1991–92 Versace show, Linda Evangelista, Cindy Crawford, Naomi Campbell and Christy Turlington, all of whom appeared in the 'Freedom' video, came out onto the catwalk together lip-synching that song. The high-octane glamour and open flouting of wealth and fame that had become synonymous with the Versace name had reached its peak.

It is widely assumed that, following Gianni's murder, Donatella was forced to take over as designer overnight. This is not, in fact, the case. As long ago as 1993, Gianni started preparing his sister for a time when he might not be around. He lost weight, appearing on the catwalk tired and emaciated to take his bows. He was, it emerged, suffering from cancer of the inner ear. For two years, while he battled with the disease, Donatella played a much more significant part in designing both Versace ready-to-wear and couture collections. Once her brother was fit again, Donatella continued to take a more active role. Their fights over each collection are legendary; Donatella insisted on trying on all the outfits herself to see whether they worked. To say she is feisty is something of an understatement. 'Nothing comes from calm,' she tells me. 'Calm is boring. Gianni was always very opinionated . . . like me.'

In the January 1998 issue of *Time* magazine, Donatella takes pride of place as one of the 'Best People' of 1997. 'For so long she has stood in the shadow of her famous older brother, Gianni. Could she, after his tragic death in Miami Beach, emerge from her grief to carry on the family tradition? At her October ready-to-wear show in Milan, celebrities and critics crowded the catwalk looking for the answer – and found it. Her clothes were youthful, fresh and oh-so-sexy. No doubt about it: Donatella, 40, who received an emotional ovation from the hard-to-please crowd, is now the most important woman in the fashion universe.'

Donatella herself is the first to admit that the 'crowd' were, in fact, in 'no way hard to please'. 'It was only two-and-a-half months since my brother died,' she says. 'I felt a lot of emotion at the first show. I felt I didn't really know what I was doing, whether it was good or bad. I knew, though, that people would forgive me everything.'

It was indeed an emotional affair. The show was dedicated to 'our brother Gianni's love of work and to our entire staff, whose incredible love and devotion were precious to him and meant so much'. Anyone ready to pounce on Donatella for having inherited the ego of a superstar designer along with the title was disappointed. She received a standing ovation for her efforts, appearing on the runway at the end of the show overwhelmed and in tears.

And yet her debut show was, as she seems well aware, not as accomplished as the second, which she showed in Milan last month. ('That time,' she says, 'I panicked.') It amply demonstrated, however, that she more than knew what she was doing, that the famous Versace glamour was in safe hands. While maintaining her brother's signatures, Donatella was, if anything, more in touch with fashion's prevailing mood. I ask her how it feels to be 'the most important woman in the fashion universe'.

'I read that!' she exclaims. 'I read it! I tell you how it feels. It feels like aargh! Who gave me this review? Please! I don't want to think like that. I like to play with power when I do clothes – to play with power and with fun. But I don't want to think like that, because I really don't think that that's how it is.'

For all the glamour of her lifestyle, the money and the power, Donatella is more practical than may be expected – down to earth, even. She says she is typically southern Italian. She has two children, Allegra and Daniel, and insists she's a very strict mother. 'You may not believe me, but I am. I like discipline with children. I like family. When Gianni was alive, every day we used to break for lunch. That's very Italian. You know, sit down together and talk about what's going on in the day. But just us. Just family. In the south of Italy, people are much more passionate, much more warm.' She talks about her children even more readily and more warmly than about fashion. 'My daughter goes to an English school,' she says. 'She thinks she's English. I keep telling her she's half Italian, half American, but she talks about the Queen every day.' Her closest friends, she says, are still those from her childhood. 'Of course, I have many friends in fashion, and that's great. I love them. But I need to have friends who are outside this world, too. It's very important to keep in touch with reality. Fashion is not reality.'

Being a mother is as important to her as working, if not more so. She talks openly to her own children about everything – 'about anything I do, about everything I see. I want them to be prepared for life. It's better if they know before what life's about. It's not a fairytale. Unfortunately, they found that out with the death of Gianni. Of course, they're special children. Apart from anything else, I take them out of school so they can travel with me. Otherwise, I'd never see them.'

Donatella is not only designer of Versace womenswear and menswear but of the Versus and Istante second lines. She describes Istante, like Versus, as younger and more moderately priced than the main line. Istante is, she says, 'for working women'. Rather than take her mind off her brother's death by immersing herself in work, however, because she is doing the job that he once did it serves as a constant reminder. It is a measure of her considerable courage that, rather than disappearing for as long as it took to grieve in private, she decided instead to continue where her brother left off. Designing eight collections a year is a tall order by any designer's standards. For a woman in Donatella's position, to be carrying it off with such aplomb is truly remarkable.

In the end, however, despite her enthusiasm, her charisma and the warmth at the heart of this extraordinarily vivacious woman, there is an overwhelming sense of loss. Frequently, as we talk, tears spring to her eyes. In the time since Gianni's death, she has had to endure not only the glare of the spotlight and the media frenzy, but also the sting of the rumours. 'It was a tragedy, what happened to Gianni. Some of the media find a way to make a business out of a tragedy. We are a company, but this is still a family,' she has said.

Donatella may be fully in possession of the fame and the fortune that goes with the Versace name, but now, for the first time, she also has to go forward on her own, without her brother, and manage without him.

'I have lost a lot of people in my family,' she says. 'My father, my mother, and now my brother. I never thought that would happen so quickly to all of them. When Gianni was alive, I was the one turning to him saying, "Don't be afraid. Why are you so nervous? You've been doing shows for years." But he was always very nervous before the show, very insecure. So I was making fun of him, trying to make him laugh. Now I find myself looking around for someone to make me laugh. There's nobody. There's all my team, of course, but the relationship between me and Gianni was so special, and I can never really have that with anyone else.'

In a way, Donatella says, she feels that Gianni is still watching over her. 'I always think, "If he can see this, does he like it?" I look up at the sky . . .' she raises her eyes to the heavens and laughs, 'you can't tell me, anyway!'

Donatella's life without Gianni has started.

16
ZANDRA RHODES

HOW WOULD YOU DESCRIBE YOURSELF AS A CHILD?

I WAS THE MOST BORING CHILD YOU COULD EVER IMAGINE. I LOVED SCHOOL – ALWAYS SAT IN THE FRONT ROW. I COULDN'T STAY AWAY.

Portrait: Andrea Vecchiato

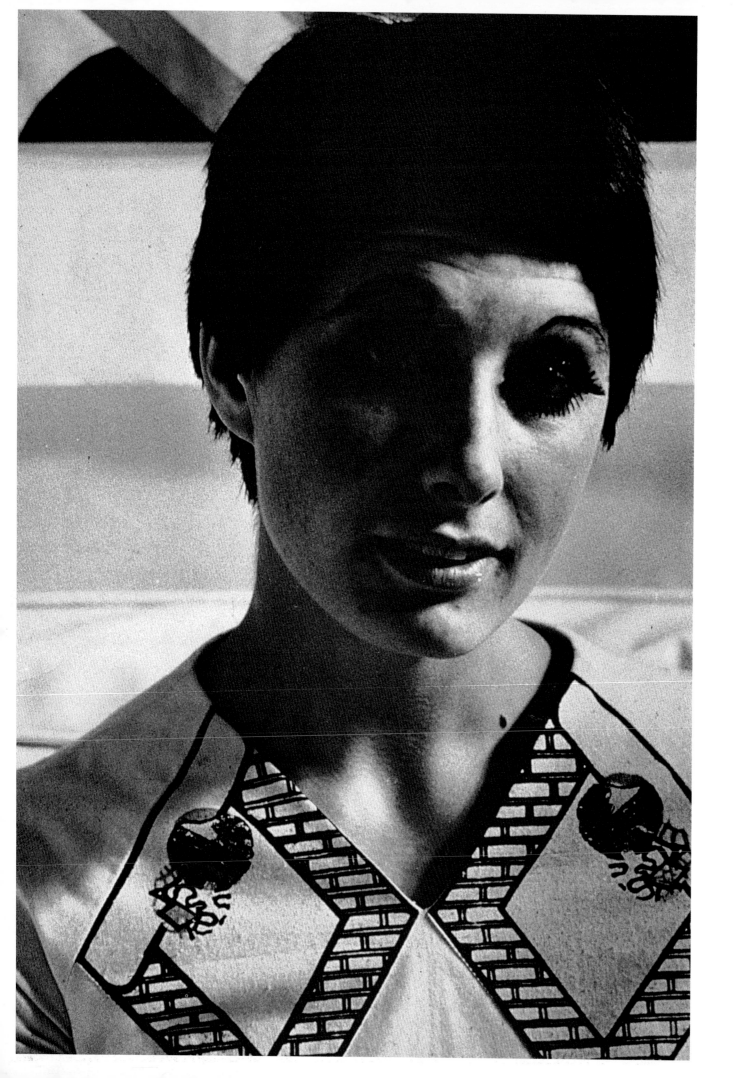

Zandra Rhodes
The Guardian Weekend magazine, 19 September 1998
Photography: Zandra Rhodes Archive

With her signature fucshia pink top-knot and make-up worthy of a kabuki player on acid, Zandra Rhodes looks, as always, on the far side of exotic – not unlike a particularly eccentric bird of paradise. That's not to say that, on this particular occasion, she couldn't benefit from a touch of grooming. Looking down at her spectacularly tatty old T-shirt and baggy tracksuit bottoms in dismay, she exclaims, 'Oooh dear, look at the state of me!' in a searing South London accent so pronounced it wouldn't be out of place in a Monty Python sketch.

'I meant to change before I met up with you. My boyfriend – who I suppose you'd describe as a sort of tycoon – is here, staying at the Savoy, so I left there this morning looking really smart, but I can't work looking smart, so now look at me!'

Her clothes this morning do indeed seem more Brick Lane than Bond Street. They're not helped by the huge bunch of keys which she wears jangling round her neck in a Prisoner Cell Block H kind of a way in case she loses them.

This sort of colourful chaos is, of course, just what one might expect from one of Britain's most enduring and inventive fashion personalities, a woman who has made it her life's mission to inspire people to dress to the nines; to dare to wear.

'It takes great courage to run around the supermarket looking like I do,' she once said. Like her clothes, she is, as they say, a one-off.

'The advantage of being female,' she confesses, woman to woman, 'is that, once you're past sixty-five, you can be a dowager empress.'

This, admittedly, is a very great thing to be.

'After the difficult part in the middle, you're allowed to be eccentric, you know, wonderful. Like Diana Vreeland or Edith Sitwell or Queen Mary. I think that, once you get above a certain age, and I'm not quite at that age yet, you get to be such a wonderful grande dame.'

Zandra Rhodes, fashion designer, loves dressing up.

'It just makes me feel better about myself,' she says. But it hasn't always been that way.

'I was the most boring child you could ever imagine!' she tells me, slapping her knees and hooting with laughter as if even she can't believe it. 'I loved school – always sat in the front row. I couldn't stay away. I believed then, and still believe now, that there's no point doing something unless you do it properly.'

Her mother, a senior lecturer in fashion at Medway College of Art in Kent, where Rhodes grew up, was, by contrast, every bit the peacock, thereby presumably planting the seed.

Legend has it that she would dress young Zandra up like the proverbial Christmas tree before taking her out when, at the last minute, her daughter would lose her nerve and bolt through the park like lightning so no one could get a close look at her.

'The only thing my parents had in common,' Rhodes says today, 'is that he was handsome and she looked gorgeous and always wore beautiful frocks. They were very into ballroom dancing.'

The prevailing feeling in the Rhodes household was that her mother had married beneath herself.

'He wasn't a bad man, they just weren't right for each other. He looked like Errol Flynn and behaved like Alf Garnett,' Rhodes says, summing things up nicely.

Since shaking off these early tendencies towards the shrinking violet, however, the designer has more than picked up where her mother left off. Her hair has gone from inky blue, through acid green, purple and, for the past few years, hot pink. She has been known to attach feathers to the ends with eyelash glue to add to the effect. She has also, famously, had her eyebrows removed ('I just felt I didn't need them any more'), then painted back on: as rows of dots and dashes like some bizarre, highly coloured Morse code, or as a single black squiggle right across her forehead.

Rhodes is similarly proud to announce that she happily plasters on bucketloads of make-up: pink circles of blusher, a different shade of lipstick on her top and bottom lip.

'I never go out without it,' she cries. It's not even unknown for her to sleep in the stuff. 'Why wash it off when someone has spent so long trying to create a look?' she's fond of wondering, not entirely unreasonably.

Zandra Rhodes, born in 1940 and brought up during the war, like many of her generation, hates waste. Like a lot of things about her, this is very British.

'I use myself as a canvas,' she explains, 'with no compromises, experimenting with my image, using cosmetics and hair to create an impact.'

And what an impact. Rhodes went from Medway College of Art to London's Royal College where she earned a scholarship to study textiles, graduating in 1962. When, out in the big wide world, large manufacturers found her textile designs too extreme for their more conservative tastes, she set to making clothes out of them herself. She opened the Fulham Road Clothes Shop at the end of the Sixties and filled it with her own work, and the rest, as they say, is history – so much so that the designer is now setting up The Zandra Rhodes Foundation, a fashion and textiles museum housing her entire archive, due to open in

Bermondsey, in the East End of London, once its creator has raised sufficient funds.

Zandra Rhodes was to the Seventies what Mary Quant was to the Sixties. Her exquisite chiffon and silk gowns in rainbow colours, often hand-painted, beaded and embroidered and worn by the highly glamorous likes of Bianca Jagger, Tina Chow, Natalie Wood, Liza Minnelli and Jackie Onassis, established her as one of the fashion icons of that decade and among the greatest fabric designers of this century.

In 1977, with the launch of her Conceptual Chic collection, American *Vogue* christened Rhodes 'the Queen of Punk'. In fact, she began experimenting with aggressively slashing silk and jersey when John Lydon was still in nappies.

Never one to miss a trick, during punk's heyday she sent out dresses full of holes of every shape and size imaginable, held together with safety pins and adorned with necklaces made of lavatory chains. Her Conduit Street shop even boasted special safety pin/brooch kits which came complete with a hand-written message from the designer herself. 'These are my special beaded safety pins,' it read. 'Yes, real safety pins! Wear them: as brooches on your collar, hanging from your necklace or chain, hanging from your earring or just hook them together for a bracelet. Have a lovely time!'

Rhodes' contribution didn't stop at dressing the so-called Beautiful People, either. Princess Anne wore Zandra Rhodes (though not a lavatory chain in sight) for her official engagement photograph, courtesy of Norman Parkinson. Princess Margaret wore one of her designs for her 60th birthday party. Diana, Princess of Wales, was similarly a great admirer.

Although she describes herself as a patriot and a royalist, Rhodes has said that if she had to find fault with the Queen, 'I'd say she doesn't dress up enough. She should be seen in her crown at all times whatever she's doing because that's what the people want.'

That's Her Majesty told, then.

It seems suitably weird, not to mention strangely fitting, that Rhodes herself is living in the building that will eventually become the museum, as if preparing herself to be the ultimate exhibition piece, a sign, if ever any were needed, of her passionate dedication to the project.

Rhodes sold her pastel pink home of over 20 years – a notorious and crumbling West London landmark – a year-and-a-half ago in order to finance the purchase of the premises which she is now frantically working on to meet the opening date. (The project has since been granted charitable status, though her application for lottery funding to put together a feasibility study was rejected.)

'The original idea happened because I'd saved all these clothes,' she explains, 'and I was shifting them around from one place to another. I was going to give them to the Victoria & Albert and I realised – although it's my favourite museum in the whole world – it's so big, you'd hardly ever get to see them. Then this building came up, and I'd already been to the charity commission because I haven't got any children and if I did a museum, I'd donate everything to the country. They told me we won't allow you to do something that's just your own work because we don't want it to be just the honour and glory of Zandra Rhodes, but we would be interested if you did something on British fashion in general. Then things started snowballing and by chance I realised I'd stumbled on something really obvious, that there isn't a museum like that in the country and it's in need of being done.'

The museum, to be designed by Mexican architect Ricardo Legoretta, will have a café and shop, a permanent collection as well as themed exhibitions and space set aside for fashion students to study and, in certain cases, reside and work. Rhodes is planning what she calls 'some sort of happening, although it might be a hard hat happening' at the space in November.

Rather disconcertingly, throughout our interview Rhodes can barely stifle her yawns. In fact, I could swear that a couple of times when we're talking, if only for a second, she falls asleep.

'As soon as I sit down for even a minute,' she says, 'I tend to drop off.'

It was, it seems, ever this way.

Iain R. Webb, fashion director of *Elle* magazine, who worked as junior design assistant for Rhodes at the beginning of the Eighties, confirms that she is famous for just this sort of behaviour.

'We'd be sitting around the table at one of her famous dinner parties,' he says, 'and someone's holiday snaps would be being passed round and then, suddenly, you'd notice they'd stopped coming. They'd stopped coming because they'd reached Zandra and she'd nodded off.'

This is hardly surprising when you consider the ferocity of the designer's work ethic.

'I work seven days a week, fourteen hours a day and there's no holiday for me that isn't actively associated with my work,' she says. She gets up at 6.30 in the morning, goes to bed at 1.30, working every day of the year except Christmas. It's not uncommon for the droves of students that come in and out of the place, working for her in some capacity or another, to make makeshift beds on the floor.

Added to this, since Rhodes met the aforementioned tycoon, one Salah Hassanein, she has been spending two weeks of the month in Bermondsey and the other two with her lover in San Diego, where she lives on the beach and dresses a coterie of fabulously grand society ladies on a private commission basis.

She has recently launched a leisurewear collection there called, appropriately enough, Zandra By Sea (!), and been commissioned by the San Diego Opera to design the costumes for a production of *The Magic Flute*, due to be staged in 2001.

'It happened that I met someone who lives in America,' she explains, matter-of-factly. 'That's the reason I originally moved there. But it's led to other things like being asked to do the opera which is something I've always wanted to do.'

If Rhodes' fantasy is still very much afloat in California, in Britain, in recent years, she has fared less well. Fashion is fickle, of course, and the recession at the end of the Eighties hit business hard. Rhodes was forced to close her London shop, her workshop in Bayswater and her factory in Olympia. Her staff was reduced from around 70 to no more than the handful of people she works with today.

Despite the fact that Gianni Versace owed the dress that launched Liz Hurley to Zandra Rhodes (openly citing her work as the inspiration), that John Galliano's most recent collection for Christian Dior had more than a touch of the Zandra Rhodes about it, and that Rhodes was turning out coats made of felt with reversed-out seams long before deconstruction had made a name for itself, Britain has shamefully neglected this home-grown designer. In a fashion world still in the throes of an extended love affair with minimalism, her over-blown and extravagant designs have been regarded as somewhat out of kilter.

Not that this appears to bother Rhodes too much: she clearly isn't one to bear grudges and still claims to feel more at home here than in America.

'I believe in this country. I don't believe I fit in anywhere else. The English are able to cope with the unusual,' she says. 'The thing about fashion, though, is that if there is any one rule it is that you know it will change. It just depends which way the pendulum swings.'

Happily, that pendulum finally looks to be swinging her way once more. This season, department store Liberty launches a capsule collection of Zandra Rhodes designs.

'Zandra has the most wonderful eye for colour and fabric,' says Angela Quaintrell, senior buyer for the store. 'The cloth is beautiful and speaks for itself and the colour is unlike anybody else's. We asked her to take all the fringing and beading off and she didn't seem to mind at all. She's an icon but she's not a number, if you know what I mean. I think that for the past few years her clothes may have been seen as too extreme, then people saw Zandra with her mad hair and everything and it all seemed very at odds with Nineties minimalism.'

Now though, and it's a great thing for British fashion, Rhodes is ripe for revival, Quaintrell says.

'Until very recently,' says Iain R. Webb, 'if you'd asked the British public to name the world's top designer, a lot of them would have given her name. She's everything you would expect of a designer – you know, changing her image every season, painting her face and dying her hair differently. Her work is all about fantasy but in a very subversive way. Today's students could do a lot worse than look to her for inspiration. She breaks all the rules but, at the same time, is very, very hard working.'

Hard working and – true to the great tradition of British fashion designers – ready to scrimp and save where necessary. It's no secret that Rhodes insists that one teabag should make two cups of tea, for example, and that dinner-party guests at her home, where the table is always laid ready to receive, are most likely to be served cauliflower cheese – hardly the staple fashion diet – rather than caviar and champagne.

On the other hand, Rhodes will always give someone in trouble a bed for the night and is famous for looking after the people who work for her on both a professional and personal basis.

'I would never say she was mean,' says Webb. 'Frugal is a better word. You know, we never had any money, so for a show we had to use last season's shoes, say, tied with ribbons so they looked completely different. For that reason, she was a truly great person to work for. She would really encourage you to make the most of yourself. It's all about using up as little of the resources as possible and relying instead on imagination. That's very much what British fashion is about.'

And if it's unbridled imagination and resourcefulness you're after, Rhodes has few equals.

'I always say I survive by ducking and diving,' she says, as she prepares herself for another afternoon's chores.

'But if, for example, I won the lottery, I would have a personal assistant and an ace hot secretary so I wouldn't have to sit here doing my own filing. I would be able to employ people to do specific things rather than having to economise with job shares. Sometimes, though, I wonder, if that happened, would we appreciate it the same? Maybe we wouldn't. Maybe we wouldn't. After all, if one's surrounded by friends and inspiration, anything can happen.'

17
REI KAWAKUBO

DOES IT WORRY YOU WHEN PEOPLE ADAPT YOUR COLLECTIONS TO SOFTEN THEIR IMPACT OR COMMERCIALISE THEM?

IF MY ULTIMATE GOAL WAS TO ACHIEVE FINANCIAL SUCCESS, I WOULD HAVE DONE THINGS DIFFERENTLY, BUT I WANT TO CREATE SOMETHING NEW. I WANT TO SUGGEST TO PEOPLE DIFFERENT AESTHETICS AND VALUES. I WANT TO QUESTION THEIR BEING.

Portrait: Timothy Greenfield-Sanders

Rei Kawakubo
The Guardian Weekend magazine, 1 March 1997
Photography: Jane McLeish. Styling: Rebecca Leary
All clothes Comme des Garçons, spring/summer 1997

What must Rei Kawakubo, the enigmatic and brilliant brains behind the Japanese label Comme des Garçons, think of her fashion contemporaries? Certainly, nobody could have predicted the media frenzy that greeted last October's ready-to-wear collections in Paris, where she has shown for more than 15 years. Rumours surrounding who would be taking over from Gianfranco Ferre at Christian Dior changed daily. Even the esteemed houses of Dior and Givenchy couldn't agree on exactly when John Galliano's and Alexander McQueen's respective appointments would be officially announced. In the meantime, the world's buyers and journalists, tempers more fashionably frayed than usual, fought longer and harder than ever to get into shows. Pounding music, bright lights and catcalling photographers whipped things up still further as the world's greatest designers showed some 1,500 spectators — more than had gathered in the world's fashion capital before — what we'd be wearing this summer. Despite the ephemeral and rarely profound nature of fashion, for the first time in years it made the front pages the world over.

In the midst of all this came Kawakubo's quiet 'presentation', which couldn't have been more at odds with the prevailing chaos around it. For two seasons now she has presented her collection away from what she describes as the 'circus' that is the official show schedule. She shows to a select group of people who she hopes will be sympathetic, or at least open, to her ideas. (It's worth noting that, since she made this decision, more than a handful of other designers have followed suit.) In the immense and sombre Musée d'Art d'Afrique et d'Oceanie, no more than 300 privileged fashion pundits were asked to form a square for this purpose. There was no catwalk. No music. The lights went up — no sunglasses required. As the first model came into view, the only things that detracted from the clothes were the whirring of the cameras and her light-as-a-feather footsteps. You could have heard a pin drop.

Viewed from the front, the slender, ankle-length dress — in pure white stretch organza with fragile cape shoulders — looked like nothing so very out of the ordinary. From behind, however, two small, kidney-shaped protuberances, positioned at the shoulder-blades like angels' wings, suggested more radical things to come. Sure enough, as the show progressed, one model after another came out with increasingly stranger, larger swellings, all under long, skinny, semi-sheer dresses — in either red, white or blue, or in winsome ginghams and gentle, fondant-coloured prints.

There were lopsided bustles, misshapen padded hips and collar bones, fat snakes coiling round waists and rib cages, and even — there is no other word for them — humps, all gracing elegant and very narrow silhouettes. Dramatic contrast came in the form of waxed, brown-paper puffball skirts and feather-light tops — pleated elaborately into Prince of Wales check, gathered into a fragile flower at the waist or pressed into myriad folds until they looked like living coral or anemones — all cut from over-sized spheres of fabric out of which limbs, necks and torsos sprouted like the stems of tropical blooms.

While the audience marvelled at the beauty of this less radical side of the show, the more extreme elements left them lost for words. Some giggled nervously (and not entirely charitably); more thought that, this time, Kawakubo had just gone too far. Few onlookers could fathom this latest offering — Quasimodo jokes filled the fashion pages of the following day's papers, and it was rumoured that one of Britain's most visionary buyers took up smoking on the spot, such was the strain on even her hitherto Comme-friendly sensibilities. Those still in tune with such radical sensibilities, however, were in raptures — this was art, living sculpture, Kawakubo's most powerful collection for years.

Almost six months later, sitting in her showroom in the auspicious Place Vendome in Paris, Kawakubo does little to illuminate the otherworldliness of her spring/summer collection, which is, even by Comme standards, perhaps the most difficult or, in Comme speak, 'strong', to date.

'Fashion right now has become rather stale,' she says in slow, deep, even tones through an interpreter (which makes her more difficult still to pin down). 'Some people focus on retro, meaning Sixties or Seventies revivals. Some people stick to very traditional classic clothing, what we call "real" clothes, very easy to put on, simple clothes. I wanted to create something that didn't belong to any of those categories, and go forward. When I sat down and thought about how to convey that message, I felt a new way of thinking was "the body becomes dress becomes body".' This is, of course, all quintessentially Comme in spirit and, it has to be said, about as clear as mud.

Even now that the dust has settled, shockwaves resonate. So extreme was the reaction to the collection that Comme des Garçons produced a leaflet, sent out by stockists to Comme enthusiasts, as if to warn them what to expect

rather than subject them to coming across it unprepared.

'Not what has been seen before. Not what has been repeated. Instead, new discoveries that look towards the future, that are liberated and lively. This is Comme des Garçons' approach to creating clothes. The spring/summer collection has arrived.'

This was announced in huge bold type. Then smaller: 'From the Sixties through the Nineties, fashion has been the driving force of the times, evoking and influencing the mood of the age with its freedom of spirit and energy. Yet in the past few years, fashion seems to have lost its direction, lost its sense of innovation and excitement, become too uniform and repetitive. Comme des Garçons has always been committed to its quest for the new and unknown, to its experiments with the not-yet-seen-or-felt, and is even more so now, when it appears that fashion is avoiding risks. Continually questioning, encouraging individuality and looking to the future – this is Comme des Garçons' approach to creating clothes.'

All this might ease things somewhat for a certain number of prospective buyers. Other less fashion-friendly souls will, no doubt, simply buy the elements of the collection without padding, or even remove it – both *Vogue* and *Elle*, to name but two, have chosen to shoot the collection *sans* lumps. But, says Kawakubo, that is highly upsetting for her. She is disappointed by such philistine actions, 'saddened' even. She understands, however, that the collection will 'certainly not be bought in great quantities.'

'If my ultimate goal was to achieve financial success, I would have done things differently, but I want to create something new. I want to suggest to people different aesthetics and values. I want to question their being.'

'I am wearing Comme today, and I adore it,' says Rita Britten, owner of and chief buyer for one of the country's most inspired designer fashion outlets, Pollyanna. 'But when I first started to buy it, it frightened me to death. In my opinion, there are only two designers who are not always tapping into something to make big bucks, and they are Issey Miyake and Rei Kawakubo.' Equally, says Britten, she buys Comme not because of how much money she is likely to make out of it, but because 'she's moving shape on. I always wear Comme as pure as I can wear it. When I put the lumps and bumps on, they will only blend in to my other lumps and bumps. Customers think I'm mad on occasion, but there are so many so-called designers who

feed women what they think they want, and Rei never does that. We need people like Rei Kawakubo, but instead of praising her, we malign her. It's just like in art. People used to hate abstract expressionism; now they all want a Jackson Pollock on their wall.'

Joan Burstein, proprietress of Browns, has bought Comme since 1981 and opened the first Comme des Garçons boutique in London in 1987. She is equally effusive in her praise for the designer. 'Her influence has been enormous,' she says. 'In nearly every other designer's collection, there's a little hint of Rei.'

Burstein is perhaps not quite so convinced by the more challenging side of the current collection. 'In the shop, it doesn't look as extreme as you might expect,' she says. 'Even with the brown-paper skirts, we've had a wonderful response.' However, of some of the padding she says, 'Rei must have wondered how women would wear it, must have wondered whether it might cause affront. Although she didn't like the criticism, she has to acknowledge it.'

Criticism aside, Kawakubo insists that, in this instance, matters commercial couldn't be further from her extraordinary mind. Because unlike many of today's designers, who rely on scene-stealing through highly impractical show pieces that are never intended to be worn but ensure media coverage, Kawakubo shows what she sells. Modify her spring/summer collection and it's almost like you're violating her person, the rigorous integrity and intensity of her ideas. That is not to say that Comme des Garçons is commercially lacking. Perhaps the most remarkable thing of all about Kawakubo is that, although she has stuck unflinchingly to her often highly challenging principles, she is now the proud owner of a business that operates in 33 countries, to the tune of $125 million wholesale a year – mostly in Japan. There are 11 collections produced in-house, including Comme des Garçons' main line collections for men and women, eveningwear and shirt lines, furniture and fragrance.

'In order to be in the position to remain radical,' she says, 'I have organised my company in a certain way.' Although Kawakubo considers her turnover to be 'not that brilliant,' the simpler lines allow her the freedom to express herself fully when it comes to showing her signature collections.

Rei Kawakubo was born in Tokyo in 1942, the daughter of a senior faculty member at Keio University. She started school while Japan was still occupied by the US army. 'By

the time she graduated,' writes Deyan Sudjic in his 1990 monograph on Comme des Garçons, 'the country had decisively emerged from the ranks of the developing world. The ferment of those years provided unique opportunities for the members of a generation that was ready to make the most of them. They enjoyed the fruits of an economic success story which enabled Japan to look at the outside world in more objective terms, to make its own creative contribution and, in the process, to assert its own identity as a mature, modern state.'

Remarkably talented products of this economic boom include not only the architects Tadao Ando and Arata Isozaki, but also three Tokyo-based fashion designers: Issey Miyake, Yohji Yamamoto and Rei Kawakubo.

After Kawakubo graduated in 1964, she worked as a stylist in the advertising department of a major chemical company, then went freelance. When she couldn't find the clothes she wanted to style, she began designing them herself.

For almost 30 years Kawakubo has been on a mission to challenge our perceptions of what is beautiful. This deceptively delicate woman – she has a will of iron, by all accounts – refuses to be swayed by passing trends, insisting instead that her creativity comes from inside, 'starting', as she has said, 'from zero'.

No wonder, then, that she objects to the crass commerciality that has over-run the world of international designer fashion. It is a measure of her talents that, even though she regularly speaks out against fashion, designers as diverse as Alexander McQueen, Jil Sander and Donna Karan all cite Kawakubo as the world's most gifted and inspirational designer.

When Yohji Yamamoto and Rei Kawakubo became the first foreign designers invited to show at the Paris collections in 1981, they made fashion history. Paris, centred as it was around the by-then bourgeois offerings of the houses of Chanel, Saint Laurent and Dior, was brought to its knees by the bleak, hard-edged solemnity of their resolutely monochromatic vision. Kawakubo sent out trousers with sweater cuffs at the ankles teamed with tunics that turned into shawls; over-sized overcoats for women, buttoned from left to right, *comme des garçons*, and – most famously – boiled, seemingly shapeless knits peppered with holes. Critics struggled to find references with which to describe the clothes, coming up – much to Kawakubo's justifiable distaste – with the term 'Hiroshima chic'. Others were more

inspired in their judgements: 'These are clothes for real women, not Barbie dolls,' said Bernadine Morris, then fashion editor of the *New York Times*.

Today, Kawakubo is dressed not in black – 'black is no longer strong and has become harder to use,' she says of the shade she and Yamamoto together put on the fashion map – but in a crisp white Comme shirt and full, ankle-length skirt the colour of sun-drenched straw. Her strict posture, sleek black bob and still, gentle, oval face only add to the mystery of the woman who insists that she would rather not talk about anything personal.

She is notoriously shy and clearly dislikes being interviewed. Yet at the same time she has the unnerving capacity of making other, less focused souls feel that they say too much and are lacking in integrity for it. Little wonder that she has by now attained guru status – her work is discussed in terms more readily associated with modern art or architecture than clothes. But she dislikes intensely being called an artist, which only adds to her reputation as a defiantly impenetrable designer.

'Rei is a fashion designer and a businesswoman,' says her press officer. 'Please don't ask her about politics.' Even the name Comme des Garçons was chosen, by all accounts, for the unlikely reason that Kawakubo 'just liked the way it sounds'. Though she has consistently subverted received ideas of how women (and indeed men) should dress – creating her own unorthodox textures and silhouettes that, more often than not, are picked up by others years, even decades, later – she insists that there is no hidden agenda.

Kawakubo is still based in Tokyo, although she travels to Paris four times a year for her shows. She is happily married to Adrian Joffe, an architect and the firm's managing director. She refuses – in the most immaculately well-mannered way – to be drawn on the subject of her private life, however, so much so that there are those who, in desperation perhaps, have labelled her a recluse.

Kawakubo smiles and insists that this is by no means the case. 'In normal, everyday circumstances, of course I'm not reclusive,' she has said, 'but this fascination with every nosy detail is so astonishing. It would be much better to know someone through that person's work. With a singer, the best way is to listen to his song. For me, the best way to know me is to look at my clothing.'

Rei Kawakubo gets up, moves silently across her showroom, and disappears without trace.

18
PAUL
SMITH

WHAT IS THE SECRET OF YOUR SUCCESS?

IT'S THAT I'VE JUST GOT ON AND DONE IT. I'VE PACKED
BOXES AND KNOW THAT VAT MEANS VALUE ADDED TAX
NOT VODKA AND TONIC. I'VE SOLD ON THE SHOP FLOOR,
TYPED INVOICES. AT SOME POINT I'VE DONE EVERYTHING
BUT I'VE ALWAYS KEPT MY HEAD ABOVE WATER
FINANCIALLY AND KEPT MY FEET ON THE GROUND.

Portrait: Gautier Deblonde

Paul Smith
The Guardian Weekend magazine, 21 February 1998
Photography: Ben Ingham. Styling: Romaine Lillie
All clothes Paul Smith, autumn/winter 1998

Paul Smith is reading aloud to me from the yellowing pages of an old hardback, recently given to him by a friend and designed to help the hapless English tourist of yesteryear grapple with the intricacies of Malay language and culture.

We begin with that time-honoured classic, clearly essential to the Englishman abroad: How To Make A Cup Of Tea.

' "Mix up a teaspoon of the sugar with the milk and give it to him," ' Smith shouts, clearly relishing the idiosyncracies of the Malay-to-English translation. 'They're so funny some of these things. Look at this: "He lives with his father at the foot of the hill." And this: "Send away some red and yellow flowers." That's really useful if you're in Malaysia, that.'

Not, on the face of it, particularly useful, it has to be said. That Smith should be interested in such things, however, is in no way out of character. It wouldn't be the least bit surprising if just these pearls of Malay wisdom eventually found their way onto the linings of future Paul Smith jackets – or printed onto Paul Smith shirts, T-shirts, socks and ties, at the very least.

There was, after all, the plate-of-plastic-noodles print that cropped up here, there and everywhere in one collection (based on those found in the windows of restaurants in Japan; to this day the original takes pride of place in Smith's office, an Aladdin's Cave of all things insane) and, more recently, huge, hyper-real moggies and saucy Fifties-style pin-ups. Neither would it be in any way out of the ordinary if the Malay book itself ended up for sale on the Paul Smith shop floor, simply because its current owner feels the need to share its strangeness with fellow interested parties.

It certainly wouldn't be out of place there. In the past few years, browsing around the designer's labyrinthine Covent Garden store, I personally have snapped up New Footie – imagine the first ever Subbuteo set, complete with an army of skinny tin football players, two tiny goals and a virulently green felt pitch – dated, impressively enough, 1957. Then there was the curious little bronze sculpture of a doleful mongrel sitting on his lonesome under a Paris street lamp, not to mention legions of clockwork robots, pristine white tubes of toothpaste with no ugly branding to wreak aesthetic havoc on minimal bathrooms and, of course, countless (Paul Smith) rubber ducks. The designer himself is not, by all accounts, averse to pulling these out of his jacket pockets at heavyweight business meetings. 'I don't know why they're called rubber ducks,' pondered the decidedly mournful voiceover to last year's Paul Smith Christmas promotional video – a riot of seasonal product placement – 'when they're always plastic.' And that's before the hapless consumer has even started on the clothes, which are, in the end, the reason why Paul Smith is famous.

'All this stuff has an interest for me because I wonder why the hell somebody has thought about it,' Smith explains. 'Why, in a world that's full of too many toys, somebody's thought of a new toy, or a product, or a book that didn't exist before. Someone once pointed out in an article that people misunderstand me because they think I have a childish approach, when in fact I have a childlike approach. I think that's right. I'm just constantly interested in stuff, and it's that enthusiasm that has kept me going.'

Such 'childlike' qualities have, by now, revolutionised menswear in this country, teaching the British male – and Eighties man in particular – that shopping for designer clothes is nothing to be ashamed of. 'Classics with a twist' is how Smith described his immaculate, sharply-cut tailoring at the time, tailoring steeped in tradition but embellished with the odd flamboyant flourish – a lime-green windowpane check on a seemingly conservative suit, for example, or a particularly loud shirt, tie or pair of socks. If the phrase seems clichéd today, it's worth remembering that Paul Smith is the man who coined it – and invented the look – in the first place.

Not content with supplying a super-chic exterior look, Smith then went on to introduce boxer shorts – printed with everything from pretty flowers to outsized polka dots – to the British male's fashion vocabulary. Suffice to say, the sorry state of their smalls will never again be the same. Then came the Filofax. 'I found this funny old address book under some railway arches at Bethnal Green,' Smith says, 'and thought it might be useful to people. They offered to sell me the company but I didn't want it. Once things are fashionable I'm not interested any more.' Oh, and if all that weren't enough, Smith also imported both matt black in general and the executive toy in particular, hot from Japan way back when. 'I was doing all that matt-black stuff long before Liberty, Conran or Heal's,' he says.

Paul Smith is now chairman of an international design company with an annual worldwide turnover of £142 million, making him this country's most financially successful designer by far. His clothes sell phenomenally well in lucrative Japan, where he has gained rock-god status, and in every major European and US city they hang alongside the best of menswear design. He is one of eight advisers on Tony Blair's design and education task force. He is the first ever fashion designer to have had an entire exhibition devoted to him (*Paul Smith: True Brit*, a show which toured all four corners of the earth). There's even a limited edition Paul Smith Mini in the pipeline – due to be launched in April – which comes in black, white and 'Paul Smith blue', the colour of one of his favourite shirts. All come complete with enamelled Paul Smith badge on the bonnet and British Isles badge on the grille. Paul Smith is, in short, a national institution. Exactly how childlike, I wonder, can all this possibly be?

'I'm okay at design, and I'm okay at business, and I'm really exceptional at neither,' he tells me. It's by no means the first time he's said it. Rather, some might say, it's his mantra – intrinsic to the charmingly self-deprecating, thoroughly British public image that Paul Smith has, for more than 25 years now, cultivated and made his own.

For the autumn/winter '98 season, Smith will show at the London collections for the first time. While his menswear will continue to be shown in Paris, the British fashion capital will be home to twice-yearly showings of Paul Smith Women, introduced four years ago in response to the fact that, throughout the Eighties, women were borrowing their boyfriends' jackets and shirts, and buying 'Smithy clothes', as the designer puts it, in small sizes for themselves.

'I was completely honest when I started the women's line,' he says, 'and said I would need three to five years, because I didn't understand this world. Also, when it started, the collection was very much about clothes for women that weren't necessarily clothes for the catwalk, that was the whole point: a nice white shirt, a suit, a jacket. It just wasn't big or mature enough, and now it is. I hope.'

It's a great moment for British fashion, because in the past Smith has made no bones about the fact that, while he may be personally steeped in British culture, he feels our fashion industry leaves more than a little to be desired. In 1992, true to his word, he turned down a nomination for the 'prestigious' British Designer of the Year Award, describing it as 'self-congratulatory'.

'There weren't that many people who could win it,' he explains, 'so it was like, "Well, it's your turn this time and it's my turn next." I couldn't see the point of having it because our industry, in terms of design, was so tiny. The awards were just an invention by the PRs to draw attention to Fashion Week. They didn't have any substance, and I don't like to be involved in things that don't have a foundation.'

This is, of course, typical of the no-nonsense, plain-spoken attitude that the designer is famous for. Fashion may love Paul Smith (he is, as anyone in its hallowed circles will gladly testify, a very nice man – this is unusual), but he has serious problems with the kissy-kissy baggage that goes with his job, and with the hype-driven, show-stopping world of womenswear in particular. 'I don't like the falseness,' he says. 'Put your hand on your heart and tell me it's not false. It's not a real world. You are attentive to somebody because you think you're going to get some gain out of it. So many designers forget that the customers are, in the end, the VIPs.'

Neither has Smith confined such criticism to fashion. Although it's hardly news that, while London might be home to the most brave and inspired creative talent in the world, it lacks the infrastructure to support it. Smith was one of the first to voice his opinions on this, too – shout them from the rooftops, in fact. Tony Blair may have made his soapbox harangues in some way official, he says, but 'I barged in on Michael Heseltine eight years ago, I've been on this crusade. The thing is to work out how, in the future, you can get the captains of industry – the CBIs and the DTIs – through education and awareness, to work out that one of the things we're good at is ideas, and that doesn't just mean designing frocks.

'We keep losing kids and their ideas because there are managers of companies and countries who understand how to handle them better than our managers do. That's just ridiculous. Vivienne Westwood is Italian-backed, John Galliano and Alexander McQueen are working in France, Moschino and Missoni use almost entirely British designers. Then you go into other industries. Head of Volvo cars, British; BMW, British design team; Bang & Olufsen, British design team; Yamaha motorbikes and Pentax Cameras, British design teams. It's like this mad brain-drain of creativity. . . '

Not, he says, that Blair's initiative is likely to change things overnight. 'We've had three meetings so far, and the idea, basically, is to talk about the whole world of creativity, rather than specifically about design, art or music. I'm personally trying to look at how to introduce things into the education system that might help future generations. One of the key things in Britain is that we have about fifteen thousand students a year coming out of design-related courses, and no more than one thousand jobs. I'd like to see design management and marketing made acceptable as a career, then more people would find employment here.' But he acknowledges, 'It's ever so hard to do. It's very hard to gauge, or even expect, specific results. It's more a nudging of ministers to make them think more laterally. Government – not this specific government, but all government – is a juggernaut, so whether it will actually work remains to be seen.'

With or without a government task force behind it, Smith says that London Fashion Week, at least, may now finally be coming into its own. 'I think things have improved massively. Designers are more organised, and they are running successful businesses. In the past, it was just hype. Important buyers would have come over, they would have given a significant part of their budget to British design, and would never have seen the clothes, or they would get them horribly late, or horribly made. Now, our designers are bringing in the goods, and I'm very happy to show here for that reason.' And very happy the much-beleaguered British Fashion Council is to have him, too.

Paul Smith was born in Nottingham in 1946 – it wouldn't be unreasonable to say that he is that city's most famous export since the infamous Sheriff. His father was a credit draper – one of a now extinct breed that made a living selling basic clothing and bed linen door-to-door – and his mother a housewife. He hated school and left, aged 15, to carry garments around a clothing warehouse. But even though he was interested in fashion ('I was fairly well-dressed by the time I was thirteen,' he says), his real love was cycling. 'I wanted to be a professional racing cyclist. I used to be in bed by nine-thirty and would cycle three hundred or four hundred miles a week. Then, when I was seventeen and doing quite well, not very well, but quite well, I fell off my bike.' He spent six months in hospital and, when he came out, discovered 'I couldn't bend my leg enough to ride my bike.' He still cycles to work, however ('that's my bike at the bottom of the stairs. Did you see it?'), but any dreams he harboured as a child of making the Tour de France were shattered.

After the accident, Smith says, he discovered socialising: 'I say socialising, I discovered the pub.' And not just any old pub, but The Bell Inn, which happened to be frequented by students from the local art school. 'I met artists and painters and fashion people and, through that, developed an interest which I think was always there, bubbling around.' At The Bell, Paul also met Pauline Denyer, who, having completed a degree in fashion design, was teaching. The two fell in love (Paul and Pauline). They have been inseparable ever since, and live together in London with Denyer's two children.

By this time, Paul Smith had become, by his own admission, every bit the dandy. 'I had a hand-made, pale-pink, single-breasted suit and red python boots. Old men used to come up to me in the street and shout: "Look at you! You look like a woman! You should be put in a dress! I fought the war for people like you!" ' Not that that stopped him – rather, this sort of reaction was positive encouragement. However, it was Denyer, now a painter, who gave him the confidence to move into fashion professionally, and, indeed, whose judgement he relied on, then as now. 'I was working as a shop assistant in a boutique – they were called that in those days, I think it was Nottingham's first – and Pauline kept telling me I had so much energy and ideas that I should do my own thing. So I worked on my day off and made extra money to start what I called a shop but what was in fact a twelve-foot-square back room.'

There he stocked various designer labels and a small number of branded Paul Smith items, designed, he is more than happy to admit, by his partner in her free time. Denyer also had 'a good job' teaching and was prepared to support him. (Later, and entirely appropriate to fashion's most famous fairytale romance, he in turn kept her while she went to art school.) For his part, Smith studied fashion at night school until, by 1974, the shop was well stocked and successful enough to extend to the high street (it still bears the Paul Smith name today). By 1976, Paul Smith was consultant to both an Italian shirt manufacturer and the International Wool Secretariat. That same year he decided to show his own line in Paris, and three years later he opened his first shop in Covent Garden's Floral Street, where he remains – he has by now colonised the whole of one side of it.

'The reason I've been so successful,' Smith says, 'is because I've just got on and done it. I've packed boxes and know VAT means Value Added Tax not vodka and tonic. I've sold on the shop floor, I've typed invoices. At some point I've done everything, but I've always kept my head above water financially, and kept my feet on the ground.'

Although it would have been easy for the designer to go down with the Eighties, it is one of his considerable skills that he, unlike others, has been able to continue doing very much his own thing while keeping up with the times.

'I was never a man of the Eighties,' he says. 'Yes, I was the guy who found the Filofax, but all I did was introduce it to the world – somebody else made it foul. I hated the greed, the corporate expansion, the people going for it. All I did in the Eighties was let it roll.' And that's exactly what he's been doing – slowly but surely expanding – ever since.

Paul Smith Women is following very similar lines to his menswear, showing 'the honesty of my menswear, with respect for the female form'. The tailoring is as accomplished as that of the menswear: jackets emphasise good shoulders, a narrow torso, a waist and breasts; trousers make legs go on forever, and Smith, who says that to begin with the collection was 'too masculine', now makes a mean pretty dress, too.

'I've hopefully picked up on my father's personality,' he says, 'and then Pauline's insistence on good quality and the construction of clothes.' He has constantly cited these two people as the most important in his life, and is visibly and touchingly unsettled by the mention of his father, who died a month ago. 'He is, was, a very down-to-earth man.

'Pauline and I have been together for a long time, and I'm happy. I'm not searching for anything, but that doesn't mean I don't want to build the womenswear into a big business – it's already worth twelve million pounds, which is bigger than a lot of other British design businesses. In the end, though, I'd like to build it into a big business with a long life, just because people like the clothes. That's it. Because they're reliable, and because people think, "If he did it, they must be all right." '

With Smith's track record, almost anything he touches, I suggest, is likely to be far more than that. Of course, such compliments embarrass him, cause him to change the subject swiftly.

'Take a look around my office,' he says. 'I've got to go off to a meeting, but look in the drawers if you like, there's some great stuff in there, take a look at anything you like.' He is noticeably more relaxed showing me around his piles of magazines, CDs, garden gnomes, wooden mice, piggy banks and general, inspired and inspirational curiosities, than he is talking about himself. In fact, despite the fact that this Boy's Own paraphernalia surrounds his every working day, he seems unable to tear himself away from it.

He shows me two talking wrist-watches, one that speaks the time in French, a second in Italian. 'Aren't they great?' He points out a Japanese poster of an enormously fat cat. 'I found it in the Tokyo subway,' he explains with pride. 'It's meant to warn people against excess.' Finally, after taking one last, loving look about him, this gangly figure of a fifty-something man disappears – sliding right down the bannisters and out of sight.

'For God's sake, grow up, Paul,' I shout after him.

'Never,' he replies.

19 JOHN GALLIANO

HOW WOULD YOU RESPOND TO THE ACCUSATION THAT YOUR CLOTHES ARE NOT MODERN?

WHAT'S MODERN? I BELIEVE WHAT I DO IS MODERN, IF YOU WANT TO CALL IT THAT. IT'S JUST SUCH AN OVER-USED WORD. MODERN TO MOST PEOPLE IN THIS GAME IS WHAT? GUCCI? OR PRADA? I THINK REINTERPRETING THINGS WITH TODAY'S INFLUENCES, TODAY'S FABRIC TECHNOLOGY IS WHAT IT'S ALL ABOUT.

Portrait: Chris Moore

John Galliano
The Independent fashion supplement, spring/summer 1999
Photography: Dmon Pruner. Styling: Sophia Neophitou

Anyone travelling to the spring/summer '99 haute couture collections in Paris last month could have been forgiven for assuming that, even with unbridled fantasy so high on the agenda, the most extreme spectacle of them all would come courtesy of John Galliano, designer-in-chief at the house of Christian Dior. This is, after all, the man who has, in the past, transformed the interior of a monolithic sports stadium, located in the particularly unglamorous suburbs of the French fashion capital, into an enchanted forest filled with 40-foot-high spruce trees. Then there was the time he installed a Manhattan rooftop scene at the normally sterile Caroussel de Louvre, official home to the Paris collections, a scene that came complete with Christian Dior trash cans – the famous CD logo was emblazoned on their battered sides – and tumbledown chimney stacks. Most famously, Galliano took over the entire Paris Opera, if you please, turning it into the world's most sartorially accomplished tea party – part English country garden, part Ballets Russes in flavour. And finally there was last autumn/winter's extravaganza: Galliano commandeered the Gare d'Austerlitz, hiring a steam train with which to ferry models onto the set and dressing the platform as a Moroccan souk, complete with exotic drapes, musclebound extras serving fresh mint tea, and burnt-orange sand floor.

This season, however, that was not to be. For spring/summer '99, Christian Dior haute couture was taken back to the salon, shown in a single room and to an audience of no more than 60 people at a time. Gone was the throbbing soundtrack, courtesy of uber-DJ Jeremy Healy, the dazzling lights, the 2,000-strong media presence – including film cameras tracking the world's most beautiful women as they walked, and spotlighting the celebrity front row – in favour of a far more restrained offering. This time round, the audience could see the clothes close up, could hear the silk rustle. What's more, in an unprecedented move, Galliano himself introduced the collection – normally he would be busy panicking backstage with the rest of them – reading nervously from a single sheet of paper and blushing coyly throughout.

The designer cited surrealism as his inspiration: 'as Dali and Cocteau understood it, with wit but always romantic'. He said he had 'always been fascinated by the relationship between Dali and his wife Gala and the power play between them for sexual dominance'. Finally, he name-checked as inspiration the surrealist photographer Madame Yevonde, famous for persuading her subjects to dress like Greek gods and goddesses. 'She came from Streatham,' said John Galliano, in a typical play between the high- and the low-brow and bringing the proceedings back to earth

with a resounding bang, adding only as he left the room with a wink: 'Just like me.'

As guests filed out afterwards, Galliano's long-time supporters marvelled at such a happening. How could the powers that be at Dior have forced such a delicate soul to stand up and face his audience? And how terrible for Galliano, who is famously shy, to have to endure such a demanding and very public ordeal. In reality, however, Galliano is rather more than a puppet. Although it is hardly news that the designer has recently, and for the first time in over a decade, been facing something of a backlash – his clothes rely too heavily on the history books, his detractors say, the spectacle threatening to overshadow the clothes – Dior executives are unlikely to be disappointed with sales figures which continue to rise.

No, this was more likely to be Galliano's way – and it was very brave – of answering his critics and ensuring they understand this current collection more fully. His eccentric appearance – particularly to non-fashion-trained eyes – and seemingly fragile disposition belie his steely motivation as a designer; to describe him as driven would be an understatement. Let's not forget that this is the man who, back in the Eighties and not long after his career started, felt that one collection in particular had been unfairly received and so took it upon himself to contact every fashion editor of note, invite them back to his showroom and talk each one through the rails individually. Although normally very gentle, criticism, as far as Galliano is concerned, is fine just so long as it's constructive but will not be tolerated if misinformed. Even his long-time collaborator Amanda Harlech (the two parted business company in 1997 – she now works with Karl Lagerfeld at Chanel) has described daring to doubt her friend thus: 'I did only once – it was a very long time ago – and I can only compare it to being hit by a massive surfing wave. His indifference is absolute.'

And now it's my turn to confront him. Over lunch at a local restaurant located close to the designer's Paris atelier, I ask John Galliano if he thinks there is any possibility that the theatrical nature of his shows might detract attention from the clothes, which are, in the end, the point. (Even at the aforementioned haute couture collection there were male models painted to look like statues, Magritte lookalikes, and lobsters for handbags.)

'I know it's a fine line,' he snaps, 'and some people think I don't need to do it but it's the backdrop to the collection, it's the way I like to design.' For Galliano, even the invitations to the show – a crimson ballet slipper, a faded love letter, a charm bracelet hidden in a Russian doll – are

an intrinsic, very carefully executed part of the whole. Even the hangers on which the clothes are displayed once they make the rails – plum-coloured velvet with John Galliano stamped on them in bright sky blue – are a thing of beauty. The designer, similarly, changes his own appearance to tie in with each collection, from swash-buckling pirate to handsome Don Juan; from besuited grand English gentleman to bleached blond rastafarian. It's all part of the message he is passionately committed to communicating.

'The venue is part of the whole story,' he explains. 'I don't have to put my name up at the back of the runway to remind people – they know where they are. I often dream of doing a show where I could give people the choice. I might do that one day, have two shows running simultaneously. One would be white light, white runway, ordinary fashion show. The other would be John Galliano. You can bet your bottom dollar that everyone would choose the theatrical presentation. There would be no one at that other show. They'd be offended to be there, call it a second rate show.'

It's true that Galliano is responsible for much of the most powerful imagery in fashion today – just one reason why the powers that be at Dior were wise to invest in him. There are those who might argue that it would be dangerous to become too accustomed to the extraordinary world he creates, disrespectful to take it for granted. I continue, nonetheless, to brave discussing the possibility of a backlash with Galliano, this time citing accusations that his clothes are no longer modern.

'What's modern?' he asks, clearly incredulous. 'I believe what I do is modern if you want to call it that. It's just such an over-used word. Modern to most people in this game is what, Gucci? Or Prada? That's just their interpretation of modern but it's still an historical take.'

In Prada's case that take has its roots in the Fifties (Formica prints and American diner chic) and, more recently, the Sixties (Couregges and Paco Rabanne). Gucci, meanwhile, has reinvented the Seventies (Mr Freedom and Halston) and the Eighties (from Miss Selfridge – at a price – to Alaïa). Perhaps, then, it's more that in our proud-to-be-minimal, functional times, Galliano's often hugely elaborate designs might seem a little out of kilter. Sportswear, admittedly, is not part of this particular designer's vocabulary. Utilitarian fashion is not on the agenda.

'Minimalism is a term that comes from the Sixties, too, actually,' Galliano's press officer, not unreasonably, points out.

'I think reinterpreting things with today's influences, today's fabric technology is what it's all about,' adds Galliano. 'You know, when I first did the bias cut, yeah, people said, "Oh, it's vintage", but then you could only get it in flea markets and even though it's the most comfortable thing you can buy. The bias cut is the most modern form of elasticity. You're cutting the fabric on the cross so it stretches without having Lycra in it. Everyone's doing it now, you can buy it in Marks and Spencer.' The reworking of the bias cut dress (think Jean Harlow in liquid silver satin) and, more impressive still, the bias cut jacket, is one of John Galliano's great contributions to contemporary fashion. Far from being unkind to women, it liberates them and, contrary to popular mythology, is not only suited to the most slender of forms.

John Galliano, 38, was born and christened Juan Carlos Antonio, in Gibraltar, his father's homeland. His mother is Spanish. 'I lived in Gibraltar until I was six,' he tells me, 'so I travelled a lot.' To go to school in Spain, for example, the designer passed through Tangiers; a hot Mediterranean influence and leaning towards exoticism comes, then, not from any fashion archive but from his earliest experiences. 'I think all that – the souks, the markets, woven fabrics, the carpets, the smells, the herbs, the Mediterranean colour is where my love of textiles comes from,' he says.

The family moved to Streatham, South London, in the mid-Sixties, where his father worked as a plumber, then later to Dulwich which remains the Galliano family homestead to this day. Galliano considers himself to be a Londoner by now. Rather sweetly, however, Gibraltar remains very proud of its most famous export: at the end of 1997, the post office there even went so far as to issue a set of John Galliano stamps printed with everything from a Belle-Epoque-inspired walking suit to a signature curvy jacket worn with skirt so short it barely grazes the thigh.

In England, Galliano attended Wilson's Grammar School for Boys where his academic performance was, by all accounts, unremarkable. Neither did he spend his time doodling the requisite fairytale princesses in maths classes or dressing up dolls and teddy bears. His mother, though, was passionate about her children's appearance and used to dress the young Galliano and his sisters, Rosemary and Immacula, in beautifully starched clothes, if only to take them, suitably primped and powdered, to the corner shop. In grim South London they must have been a sight for sore eyes.

'I don't think people in England understood where I was coming from,' he says of his early days in this country, 'and I certainly didn't understand where they were coming from. It was quite a shock, coming from that sort of family, that sort of colour. My mother brought it with her on the plane though, you know, the religious aspect, and all that was still with us when we were at home.'

The fact that the designer was brought up a practising Catholic, in particular, set him apart from his contemporaries, he says.

'They were Church of England, I was Roman Catholic. That's a big difference, you know. I was an altar boy, a choir boy. I did my confirmation in England. I am still religious. I believe in God. I don't go to church regularly any more. The last time I went was last Christmas. I went there with my trainer. We jogged there. Jogged to Notre Dame and then out again. It was really cool – really beautiful.'

It wasn't until he moved to the City of East London College, aged 16, to study for his O and A levels that John Galliano discovered the arts and met people 'a bit more like me'. From there he went to Central Saint Martins and, as they say, a star was born.

'I was a very good student,' says John Galliano, modestly. 'Sheridan Barnett was my tutor. I worked very hard. I was really into what I was doing. I was always in the library, sketching endlessly.' He also did work placements with Stephen Marks – now the brains behind French Connection and one of the most influential men in commercial British fashion – and the late Tommy Nutter, and worked in the evenings as a dresser at the National Theatre.

John Galliano's degree collection at Central Saint Martins was one of the century's great fashion moments. Les Incroyables, it was called, and Galliano says that dressing a production of *Danton* at the National by night planted the seed. There were jackets worn upside down and inside out – this was 1984: deconstruction wasn't even part of the fashion lexicon – and hugely romantic organdy shirts that wouldn't look out of place on the designer's runway to this day. Galliano worked on every last detail, from accessories including magnifying glasses, smashed to pieces by the designer himself to look just so, to the ribbons sewn onto the insides of coats.

'I was just so into that collection,' Galliano says. 'It completely overtook me. I still love it. I love the romance, you know, charging through cobbled streets in all that amazing organdy. There are a lot of things in that collection that still haunt me. Afterwards, of course, I realised that something had gone down.'

Sally Brampton, then fashion editor of *The Observer*, was there to witness Galliano's degree show. 'The entire audience got to its feet,' she says. 'The talent was just so obvious. You know when you see something – and it's very rare – where the talent is just shining through.'

Joan Burstein, proprietess of Browns, agreed, so much so

that she immediately gave over a window of the store to the designer.

'Everything happened so quickly,' says John Galliano. 'She cleared the window that afternoon, I think. Then she invited me to come down to the boutique to meet the customers and sell the collection. Diana Ross walked in, everything was just flying off the rails.' Burstein then forwarded Galliano money to go out and buy fabric to make more and supply increased demands. 'I went to Notting Hill Gate and bought some furnishing fabrics. Luckily, my parents were away, so it was alright to turn their sitting room into a mini-factory.'

Of course, the down-side of being the Next Big Thing – and it would not be unfair to say that John Galliano was, well, the biggest Next Big Thing of them all – is that you are forced into the limelight when not yet ready for it.

'It put an enormous amount of pressure on me,' he admits today. 'You have to do all your growing up in public. You make a fool of yourself in front of people you still have to work with today. So what? I'm human. It was all part of growing up.'

People still bemoan the lack of solid infrastructure in this country so necessary to supporting our young designers. John Galliano's story is the classic example of this: an award-winning designer, so uniquely talented, so unanimously revered but unable, nonetheless, to secure long-term financial backing. In the ten years following his graduation, the designer was faced with two backers withdrawing their support and several seasons in which he couldn't afford to show at all. For a man who lives for his work, this must have been particularly galling.

'You know, I've always had good friends,' he says. 'And in my darkest moments they would take me out, look after me a bit. But no, I've always seen it as a positive challenge. I had to do it, after all. I had no choice. I love what I'm doing. I love the very act of creating. Then and now, it was all I could do.'

In the early Nineties, Galliano, disillusioned by the difficulties of running a fashion business in this country, moved to Paris. There, almost penniless, he slept on friends' floors, cobbling together a first collection by calling in favours, only to find that, despite critical acclaim, he was so broke by the time the next one came round that he was in trouble once again. Help came in the form of the then, as now, hugely powerful Anna Wintour, who, in an unprecedented attachment between editor and designer, took Galliano under her wing. The next time it looked like he was heading for financial difficulty, Wintour used her considerable influence to find him a backer (investment bank Paine Webber International) and even a venue (the crumbling mansion of the legendary socialite Sao Schlumberger). Still it was a scramble – perhaps the most lovely scramble of all time. The invitation was a rusty key. Kate Moss, Christy Turlington and Naomi Campbell worked the show for love rather than sackloads of money. There were only 17 outfits put together at the last minute and entirely in black – several bolts of black fabric were all that Galliano could afford. But what outfits. The show was a monumental success – John Galliano's reputation as one of the latter part of the century's great designers was, in no more than a few minutes, sealed.

'I don't think John has changed one iota since then,' says Sally Brampton. 'There's only ever been one thing important to him and that is his work. Firstly, there's the technical aspect – he's always been obsessed with getting things right technically. Second, there's the show. He's a truly great showman, the greatest 3-D image-maker alive. It is very important that people understand that.'

One man who clearly understood it to the full was Bernard Arnault, president of the mighty fashion conglomerate LVMH (Moët Hennessy Louis Vuitton). It was a brave move on Arnault's part – if, in retrospect, an obvious one – when he decided in October 1995 to install John Galliano as designer-in-chief at the house of Givenchy. Galliano might have seemed like a young upstart to the largely archaic French fashion establishment, but French fashion – and haute couture in particular – was in need of a fix of bright young blood. Galliano's grasp of what was happening on the street coupled with his technical virtuosity made him more than man enough to exploit the skills of the most accomplished craftspeople in the world, to reinterpret their handiwork, dragging it, albeit kicking and screaming, into the 21st century.

The appointment of Galliano to Givenchy was one of the greatest fashion publicity coups of all times. Rumours began circulating months before anything was formally announced. By the time it actually happened the media had reached such a frenzy that before Galliano had designed a single outfit, Givenchy was back in the headlines once more.

'I really couldn't tell anyone about it,' Galliano says. 'Not even my mum and dad. If I told one person, that was it. It's like, you always tell your best friend, don't you? But then your best friend tells their best friend. It was just too scary.'

With Galliano installed at Givenchy, it wasn't long before still more rumours came to the fore. Alexander McQueen was to take over there, leaving Galliano free to move across to Christian Dior – perhaps the most auspicious

fashion house of them all. Fashion apoplexy ensued.

Galliano is dressed today in chunky knit sweater and dark denim jeans. On his feet he is wearing over-sized Nike trainers, on his head a jaunty black beret, cutely set off by a large pair of hoop earrings. He was, he says, dressed in a similar vein when he received the phone call from Monsieur Arnault one Friday night almost a year to the day after taking over at Givenchy.

'It was amazing,' he says, clearly still overwhelmed. 'I nearly fell off my chair. I thought I'd fucked up, thought I'd done something really bad at Givenchy. I got this phone call on Friday at six o'clock asking me to go to Monsieur Arnault's office. I thought, "Oh shit". I was totally unprepared. I had the wrong shade of toenail polish. I was wearing Scholls. Clack, clack, clack. There was no way I could get out of it, though. I had to go. And that was when he offered me the job and, I mean, I nearly fell off my chair.' He laughs and almost punches the air. 'Yes!'

John Galliano now designs no less than 12 collections a year. The Dior boutique – it's not unlike a John Galliano superstore – is packed full of everything from Christian Dior wedding dresses to petticoats, shoes, bags and, of course, cosmetics and fragrances. I visited just before Christmas to find the place positively heaving with people of all ages queuing to buy into the image that John Galliano had created. The designer is now, as he always has been, a man possessed. And it shows.

Going back to his studio after lunch, he takes time out to give me a guided tour of the garden located in the forecourt. Even this bears his signature. 'Look at this little fountain,' he says, pointing. 'And over here, where we've planted these bulbs.' Lush greenery, a sparkling waterfall and even a gazebo – and all in a not particularly salubrious part of polluted central Paris. 'We wanted it to have a *Midsummer Night's Dream* feel,' says the designer.

I ask Galliano how he would like to be remembered. 'I suppose as a romantic,' he says. And John Galliano is fashion's great romantic – from the clothes he designs and his colour-rich background to his charmed rise to fame which reads not unlike the finest of fairytales. But this is one designer determined not to retreat into his ivory tower, determined not to be dismissed as a mere producer of costume. That, perhaps, is why any recent criticism has irked him.

'There's still so much to do,' he says. 'So much to work on. There's the perfume, the stores. I'd like to do menswear . . . '

Rest assured, Galliano is a power house. If he sets his mind to it, anything is possible. It will all be done – and beautifully.

20
JUNYA WATANABE

ARE YOU BOTHERED THAT SOME PEOPLE MIGHT FIND YOUR CLOTHES DIFFICULT TO UNDERSTAND?

I DON'T EXPECT EVERYONE TO UNDERSTAND MY WORK. IT WOULD BE IDEAL IF THEY WOULD WEAR MY CLOTHES, BUT I WOULD BE SATISFIED AND HAPPY TO KNOW THAT THEY FEEL SOMEWHAT INSPIRED BY OUR WORK.

Portrait: Masayuki Hayashi

Junya Watanabe
The Guardian Weekend magazine, 15 August 1998
Photography: Robert Wyatt. Styling: Lucy Ewing
All clothes Junya Watanabe, autumn/winter 1998

It can't be easy being the publicist for Japanese designer Junya Watanabe. Part of the Comme des Garçons stable – Rei Kawakubo launched and continues to support his twice-yearly collections – he is, I am reliably informed, even more shy than his mentor. (Anyone who's had the privilege of interviewing Kawakubo will know that that's very shy indeed.) In fact, Watanabe 'hates' interviews. Instead, he has finally been persuaded to send out 'statements' regarding his work. Failing that, the hapless interviewer is encouraged to fax a list of questions to the designer, who lives in Tokyo – travelling to Paris only for the collections – and is therefore hardly accessible at the best of times. Three days after sending my fax, and: 'Here are the answers from Junya,' writes the Comme des Garçons PR. 'As usual, he did not say much.' Not what a journalist wants to know, really, and, as it turns out, something of an understatement.

SF: What is the inspiration behind your current collection?
JW: I thought something new might be born if I stopped structuring clothes in the conventional or traditional way.
SF: Do you have a certain woman/women in mind when you design your collections?
JW: No.
SF: Do you expect your clothes to be worn as complete outfits?
JW: We propose complete outfits from head to toe. But what matters most is the taste of each individual who wears them. It must be her way of expressing herself. She should be ultimately responsible for it.
SF: Are you responsible for styling your collections?
JW: I am responsible and do everything.
SF: Is there any political message behind your designs?
JW: None.
SF: Would you describe yourself as unconventional?
JW: No.

SF: Who are the designers you admire?
JW: I respect and thank Rei Kawakubo.
SF: Do you take any notice of trends?
JW: I do, but only after each collection is finished.
SF: Are you bothered that some people might find your clothes difficult to understand?
JW: I don't expect everyone to understand my work. It would be ideal if they wear my clothes, but I would be satisfied and happy to know that they feel somewhat inspired by our work.
SF: Is there a chance that you might develop licensing deals – fragrances, second lines – in the future?
JW: I don't know.
SF: Do you think there is a distinctly Japanese aesthetic behind your work?
JW: Yes, of course.
SF: Do you think that it is, for the most part, Japanese designers who push fashion forward?
JW: I know that there are many excellent designers in other countries such as the UK and Belgium. But what counts is the approach of each individual designer and not his/her nationality.
SF: Do you find designing clothes easy or difficult?
JW: I find it difficult.
SF: Would you ever do anything other than design clothes?
JW: No.
SF: Why do you design for women rather than men?
JW: There is no reason for it.
SF: What is your ambition?
JW: I most want to be able to create what I like and the way I like, and will be satisfied with that.
SF: What makes you happiest?
JW: At the moment I feel very happy that people take interest in what we have worked hard to create.

All of which tells you almost nothing about the designer

as a man, and not all that much about his clothes. Junya Watanabe, it seems, is (impressively enough) even more elusive than the aforementioned Kawakubo; even more elusive than the famously elusive Belgian designer Martin Margiela. Junya Watanabe is, therefore, without question, quite the most elusive fashion designer in the world.

Here's what is known about him: Watanabe is 36 years of age, and went straight to Comme des Garçons after graduating from Tokyo's Bunka Fashion Institute in 1984. In 1987 he began designing the Comme des Garçons Tricot line. In 1992 came his first own-label collection, still supported by the Comme umbrella. It's an unusual arrangement. He continues, without creative interference, to be backed by the label to this day, and has 19 retail outlets in Japan and some 30 in the US and Europe.

'It's his business,' Kawakubo has said of her protégé. 'Whatever Junya does, I don't interfere.'

For his part, Watanabe is sweetly modest about his role, and about Kawakubo's support, for that matter. All he learned at fashion school, he says, 'was how to use a needle and thread and a sewing machine. Everything else I learned at Comme des Garçons.'

Although he has now achieved cult status in the world of designer fashion, particularly avant-garde designer fashion, Watanabe's appearance only adds to the mystery surrounding the man. Besuited, bespectacled and remarkably conventional on the face of it (part executive, part Japanese schoolboy: on his feet he wears trainers rather than brogues), he seems a million miles away from what one has come to expect from a cutting-edge designer. His clothes, however, speak for themselves.

Following in the footsteps of Kawakubo and her contemporary Yohji Yamamoto, Watanabe is the latest Japanese designer to explore new concepts with both cut, fabric and styling, remaining, it seems, studiously out on a conceptual limb and wilfully oblivious to any prevailing trends. Back in 1995, amid a Paris fashion establishment locked into minimalism, Watanabe thought nothing of sending out an acid-bright selection of PVC clothing that resembled a pick-and-mix bag of sweets: Ellen Barkin and Björk became devotees. The following season, for no particular reason other than that, presumably, he felt like it, Watanabe's collection was gothic. To a deafening and appropriately grim Jimi Hendrix soundtrack, pale-faced, heavily tattooed models traipsed down the runway in black leather with zips in strange places, and (also black) boiled wool. There followed a cleverly commercial collection (for Watanabe, at least) of half dresses, conventional from the front, non-existent at the back, and worn over trousers. Jewel-coloured jackets, cut in myriad origami pleats and folds, fell neatly over narrow floral skirts, and Watanabe made the pages of British *Vogue*, along with just about every other fashion glossy worth its salt.

For the autumn/winter '98 season, once again Watanabe clearly started with a blank page and (also clearly) had more than the trend-forecasters to thank for his most startling offering to date. According to the designer, the collection is based on 'unconstruction'. Sheets of wool melton are wrapped around the body like pleated schoolgirl skirts or kilts, and suspended from coils of wire. These are teamed up with men's cotton shirts worn over the top or beneath, their hems often trailing almost to the floor.

True, it's not for the faint-hearted: Watanabe is evidently not aiming to poach an Armani- or Calvin Klein-friendly clientele. But as an exercise in pattern cutting it stood out brightly and beautifully among the rest. And if you're at a loss as to how to wear it, at the Comme des Garçons shop in London's Brook Street, staff are more than happy to give lessons (long and complicated lessons) on how any one particular outfit may or may not be put together. Proof, if any were needed, that you should under no circumstances try this one at home.

21
CLEMENTS RIBEIRO

HOW WOULD YOU DESCRIBE YOUR SIGNATURE STYLE?

WHAT WE DO NOW IS A BIT ODD, A BIT CLUMSY, BUT IT HAS SOPHISTICATION AS WELL. WE LIKE THAT, YOU KNOW, THINGS THAT ARE SMART. BECAUSE EVERYTHING'S GETTING MORE AND MORE RAGGED. THERE'S SO MUCH BAD TASTE AROUND. WE LIKE OUR CLOTHES TO BE SMART AND ELEGANT.

Portrait: Chris Moore

Clements Ribeiro
The Independent on Sunday Review magazine, 13 February 2000
Photography: Glen Erler. Styling: Sophia Neophitou
All clothes Clements Ribeiro, spring/summer 2000

Suzanne Clements and Inacio Ribeiro are like the Terry and June of British fashion – in the most glamorous way imaginable, of course. Ask Ribeiro to summarise his signature style while training at Central Saint Martins, where the two first met, for example, and suffice it to say that bickering, in the way that only happily married couples know how, merrily ensues.

Inacio Ribeiro: It was very experimental, each thing was completely different.
Suzanne Clements: [Deadpan.] It was over the top.
IR: [Ignoring his wife's contribution entirely.] I played with colour and texture and fabrics. You know, the fabrics we have in Europe that we take for granted, for me, coming from Brazil, were just dazzling.
SC: It was over-decorated.

Inquire whether, when they first came across each other back in 1988, in a college corridor, it was love at first sight, and don't be surprised if you emerge none the wiser.

SC: I met him on our very first day at college, when everybody's new. I was, like, 'hi'. And he's from Brazil. And I'm, like, 'oooh, are you from Rio?' And he says, 'no'. And I'm, like, 'shit'. Still, I used to really like him. Nice guy, shame about the work.
IR: She hated the way I dressed too, my haircut, my glasses . . .
SC: God almighty, it was so bad. It was like nasty leftovers from Brazil. So, I moved in with him and was, like, 'ditch your wardrobe'. Don't you think women always do that? It was like a gradual makeover.
IR: [Resigned.] She's very good at that.

As for establishing their age . . .

IR: How old are you, Suzy? My answer very much depends on that.
SC: I can't remember.
IR: Put it this way, I was a mature student.
SC: You weren't that old.

We meet, just before Christmas, at the couple's West London home, a triumph of what can perhaps best be described as shabby chic.
'People always want to do interiors features on us,' says Clements, 'but we live out of boxes so I can never understand why.'
Huge white rooms, bare, untreated floorboards, over-stuffed sofas, fairy lights surrounding large living room windows, and baby Hector – looking suitably dapper dressed in Clements Ribeiro cashmere knickers from the new childrenswear range – running amok, all add to the atmosphere of ordered chaos, presided over just now by Clements' own mother, who, in contrast to her surroundings, is more plain chic than shabby, it has to be said.

It's cold outside and Clements is in the kitchen, warming her hands round a cup of steaming sake. 'I've never believed in wearing only our own clothes,' she says. 'I don't like it. It's like musicians only wanting to listen to their own music, don't you think? Like Paul McCartney only listening to Paul McCartney. It's a bit sick.'

Her look *du jour* is a pale jade cashmere V-neck from the couple's first ever collection, a jewel-coloured bias cut, knee-length skirt (also Clements Ribeiro) and a pair of battered old Prada slingbacks, circa 1996 – beige and, well, slightly off, if in the distinctly elegant Prada/Suzanne Clements mould. 'I need to get a haircut,' she moans, tugging on her just-too-short-to-qualify-as-bobbed hair that looks, today, as always, immaculate.

'When I was pregnant, I couldn't drink at all. I just craved banana milkshakes – banana and Jack Daniels milkshakes.'

It seems only churlish to point out that, to most people's minds, an insatiable desire for Jack Daniels milkshakes is hardly your average teetotaller's wont.

'We should go round the corner and eat something, Suzanne,' says Ribeiro, clearly exhausted at the end of a hard day and desperately attempting to chase the missus out to a restaurant next door. 'I'm starving.'

All while talking to me ten-to-the-dozen, attempting to say goodbye to her family and searching in her handbag for her keys, she shrugs on a tweed Helmut Lang overcoat (his) and, happily anticipating dinner – 'they do the best potato skins in the world, do you like those?' – we close the door behind us and go out into the night.

Suzanne Clements and Inacio Ribeiro – the husband-and-wife team responsible for the Clements Ribeiro label – are the most fêted design duo in British fashion. After considerable research, it can be reliably confirmed that he was born in 1963 in Itapecerica, Brazil; she, in 1963, Surrey, England. They met at Central Saint Martins in 1988, graduated with first class honours in 1991 and were married in 1992. At college, she discovered discipline in minimalism – 'now it's so everywhere, you get it in Jigsaw, but then everyone was into Galliano'. He, meanwhile, freed of the commercial restraints of making a living for seven years designing mainstream collections in his native Brazil, took the opportunity to run wild and revel in the riot of colour and texture at his fingertips for the first time. But love, it seems, can conquer such creative divides. It could even be said that the success of the Clements Ribeiro label lies in just this surface incompatibility; in the fact that, in the case of Suzanne Clements and Inacio Ribeiro, opposites really do appear to attract.

It is a creative collision that has been much emulated since the label's launch. Back then, the brave Clements Ribeiro formula of mixing rainbow-striped sweaters with windowpane check, tartans, paisley prints and kooky florals; of throwing naïve embroideries and arts and crafts techniques in with strict tailoring; of drawing from influences as diverse as Victoriana and punk; of schoolgirl and Stepford wife, was nothing short of revolutionary.

When the label first launched, London fashion veered between the outlandishly power-dressed and in-your-face sexy, and the conceptual but rarely commercial. Internationally, fashion was a very serious business: if you weren't dressed from head-to-toe in one of the so-called 'intellectual' labels – Martin Margiela or Ann Demeulemeester, to name just two – or in shades of loosely structured working woman greige, you were nowhere. The mix and match aesthetic that Clements Ribeiro have come to symbolise – and which is now seen everywhere from Tokyo to Milan, and from the pages of *Vogue* to the Great British high street – wasn't on the map.

'I took Suzanne to New York for the first time,' says Ribeiro. 'And she couldn't find nice, posh clothes anywhere. All the clothes were just so extreme, everyone was just too fashion victim for words. From the start, there have been two basic elements running through our work. The first is the mix and match bohemian thing. And the other is the conservative. We have a love for bourgeois fashion.'

'I like things a bit square,' Clements confirms.

This is true, perhaps now more than ever.

'What we do now is still a bit odd, a bit clumsy, but it has sophistication as well,' says Clements. 'I like that, you know, things that are smart. Because everything's getting more and more ragged. There's too much bad taste around. We like our clothes to be smart and elegant.'

Clements Ribeiro's signature is indeed smart and elegant, if always slightly askew. Most importantly of all, however, it is also unashamedly luxurious, with the emphasis firmly on precious fabrics and workmanship, embellishing a sophisticated, if kooky, cut. With this in mind, their main line collection aside, Clements Ribeiro's greatest contribution to fashion so far, and one that reaches far beyond the international catwalks, is to have singlehandedly reinvented cashmere and made it the yarn to see and be seen in.

'Suzanne always wanted to wear cashmere,' says Ribeiro, 'but she could only find it in the most hideous cuts. So she bought an extra, extra petite sweater at Bergdorf Goodman and it was her first cashmere ever.'

'I look at it now,' adds his wife, 'and it's like, "give it away". It's this big, baggy thing.'

'So we did all the stripes, in the very bright colours,' says Ribeiro. 'Nobody used to treat cashmere in that way. . .'

The rest of the world wasn't slow to catch on, however. The well-heeled fashionable wardrobe would these days be sadly depleted without at least a handful of delicate, cheerfully coloured cashmere knits to brighten up a dreary day. In 1996, Clements Ribeiro launched its cashmere range, spin-offs of which can now be found everywhere from Gap to a more reasonably priced capsule collection designed by their own fair hands for Top Shop.

'I love Top Shop,' says Clements. 'I love the whole concept. When you go down those escalators, it's a real buzz, don't you think? It's really raw fashion, in one day, out the next, and it never tries to be anything other than it is.'

'Top Shop does help us with cash flow black holes,' says Ribeiro. 'It's very hard for such a small company to keep afloat when the overheads are so huge. It's also great that our vocabulary reaches a larger group of people. And it enables our signature looks to become stronger. We really try to focus on our strengths, on our key basic looks, regardless of seasons and trends, like stripy knits, say, or tartan . . .'

It is rare, particularly in Britain, for designers of such a high-profile label to be so unaffected by the pretentions of high fashion, so unashamedly happy to adapt their creative talents to suit more plainly commercial needs. For this reason, Clements Ribeiro are one of the few design teams to bridge the gap between the mainstream and the supremely fashionable; between that which young designers might think women want to wear and how they actually choose to dress. In this they appeal, pretty much uniquely, to both the more accessible glossy magazine sensibility and the avant-garde alike. Small wonder, then, that the label today has a worldwide wholesale turnover of £3 million (that's £9 million retail), which is substantial, particularly by British standards.

So, does continuing success mean a new likemindedness and even harmony developing between the happy couple?

'Of course. We do have a common ground,' says Ribeiro, smiling, 'in the sense that both of us love naïve art, for example, we also both love rough edges. But whereas Suzanne tends to be ninety per cent raw, I'm twenty per cent raw. We used to fight a lot more but after more than ten years together we have covered a lot of common ground and that levels us.'

Some things never change, however. I ask Clements Ribeiro how their working together breaks down on a daily and entirely practical basis.

IR: I tend to organise the research and ideas of the collection.
SC: I do more of the spontaneity.
IR: I like to spend ages fussing over things and analysing them.
SC: I'm, like, 'let's just do this – right now'.
IR: I have an obsession with precision, perfection . . .
SC: And I like a bit more of a mess.

The future, for the time being, then, is messy – messy in the obsessively perfect way that only Clements Ribeiro know how.

22 JEAN PAUL GAULTIER

WHY HAVE YOU CHOSEN TO USE UNCONVENTIONAL MODELS – A SILVER-HAIRED ELDERLY LADY FOR YOUR FIRST FRAGRANCE CAMPAIGN, FOR EXAMPLE, OR MALE AND FEMALE MODELS CAST FROM THE STREET?

YOU KNOW, FASHION CAN BE QUITE FASCISTIC. SOME GIRLS ARE LONG AND THIN AND THEY ARE JUST PERFECT LIKE THAT, OTHERS HAVE BIG BREASTS AND BUMS AND, YOU KNOW, THAT IS BEAUTIFUL TOO. PEOPLE HAVE TO BE AS THEY ARE. AND IF THEY FEEL GOOD AND COMFORTABLE LIKE THAT THEY WILL BE BEAUTIFUL.

Jean Paul Gaultier
The Guardian, Friday Review, 6 June 1997
Photography: Fifth Element/Kobal

Jean Paul Gaultier's peroxide blond crop is resting on a nest of puffed up, chintz-covered pillows in his decidedly genteel suite at Duke's Hotel, St James's, London. Clad in the requisite Breton T-shirt, narrow-legged trousers and ugly shoes – no kilt today, sadly – he points at some bottles on a dresser in one corner and announces:

'They are very nice, these bottles of water, no? They look like bottles of vodka, I think. I woke up this morning feeling very thirsty, looked at them and thought to myself: "Oh my God! Vodka! You Engleesh!" Hahahahaha.'

Gaultier is in London visiting his 'British cherms', as he most famously described those who live here, to talk about his collaboration with the film director Luc Besson on the science fiction blockbuster *The Fifth Element*. A huge man, and every bit as cartoon-like in real as in TV life, he has nothing but good to say of the director – all while strangling the English language, rendered barely intelligible by his equally exaggerated French accent, of course.

'I met Luc in Cannes, at a party for Madonna,' he says. Gaultier famously created the costumes for the Blonde Ambition tour, filmed live for *In Bed With Madonna*. 'And I was knowing his movies and liking very much his visual point of view. So, when he asked me to do this, I was very excited. It was like an adventure because I had to fit into one story that was not my story. I was not the boss. I had one boss – Luc. This is very good, no?'

Gaultier is also happy to confirm today, with the apparently childlike enthusiasm that is as much his signature as the crop, that Bruce Willis (just like a bottle of water that looks like a bottle of vodka?) is also 'very nice. He knows very well his body. He is very sexy and it is not difficult to make him even more sexy. I would say to him, so, perhaps we should take these trousers in a little here [he points to the back of his right thigh], and he was knowing exactly what I was speaking about. He understood very well which part of his anatomy I wanted to emphasise. Hahahahahaha.' Gary Oldman, meanwhile, isn't just nice, he's 'great, great, great. Fantastic. He was frightened of nothing'. This includes the Hitler haircut and unflattering disc of Plexiglas welded to the side of the actor's face throughout the film, presumably. Gaultier shakes his head in admiration. 'He's very impressive, really.'

Besson has said that Gaultier worked on every last detail of the film, putting the finishing touches to each extra with his own fair hands. The film's climax in particular – think Covent Garden Opera House goes *Lost In Space*, all presided over by an intergalactic diva clad in ice-blue latex so tight-fitting it looks like porcelain – has Gaultier's heady mix of classic glamour and street-inspired subversion, of *fin de siècle* elegance and sex-shop chic, stamped all over it.

'But you cannot see it!' Gaultier wails, bemoaning the length of the scene in question. 'It's only three minutes long! You cannot see the clothes!' No need to ask Gaultier what he thinks of feral beauty Milla Jovovich, meanwhile. Clad in nothing but bandages, with her alabaster complexion, feline grace and slender frame, she is, quite simply, the stuff fashion designers' dreams are made of.

While model-turned-actress Jovovich and her like might loom large in Gaultier's dreams, they are not the only ones. This is, after all, a designer who has made something of a career out of championing less conventional concepts of beauty, choosing his own face to advertise the launch of his first fragrance before, in a matter of seconds, it mutated into that of a very lovely silver-haired lady, and casting male and female models from the street for his shows long before any other designer had dreamed of such a thing.

'You know, fashion can be quite fascistic. It's like when they say girls who are shapely are out of fashion, it's just stupid. Some girls are long and thin and they are just perfect like that, others have big breasts and bums and that is beautiful too. People have to be as they are. And if they feel good and comfortable they will be beautiful.'

Of his first show in Paris in 1976, he says, 'I didn't like some of the classical models who were so obviously just doing their jobs, like functionaries. You know, "I'm wearing fur so I touch the fur to make it seem sensual", I hated that kind of *savoir-faire*. And I saw, in the street, some nice girls, nicely dressed, but in their own way – fleamarket clothes, dark red lips – and I thought these girls, they love fashion, they love to dress up, maybe it's better that I show this kind of girl. And I did. And it shocked some people in the beginning, but some others liked it.'

More than 20 years on, Gaultier – whose sartorial accolades by now include putting the style back into the city pinstripe, employing underwear as outerwear, and making tattoos and body piercings acceptable on the Paris catwalk – continues to challenge the fashion establishment's idea of good taste. In January, he was invited into the hallowed world of haute couture for the first time and promptly sent out not only couture for women but also for men. 'I am all for equality and gender, hahahaha! So I think if women 'ave it, why don't poor men. Poor things.'

Joking aside, the collection, presented in the élitist confines of the salon, complete with old-school couture presentation voiceover – 'numéro un . . . robe de crêpe de Chine noire . . . etc., etc.,' – showed the longer-established and more venerable houses of Paris a thing or two. Quietly, and without fanfare, Gaultier brought the archaic world of haute couture forward to suit women – and indeed men – of the 21st century, showing the most immaculately cut long, lean tailoring and delicate evening gowns but also more modern garments: the breton T-shirt reworked into a sinuous knitted dress (for her), say, jewel encrusted denim suiting (for him).

Then, in April, quietly, and only weeks before Naomi Campbell not-so-quietly made the headlines accusing the fashion industry of racism, Gaultier's ready-to-wear show featured entirely black models – in protest, it emerged later, against the French government's tightening of immigration laws.

'To be honest,' he explains, 'two months before the show I was thinking of trying to conjure up the spirit of Harlem in the 1940s, so I already knew I was going to use a lot of black girls, maybe seventy per cent. Then, two weeks before the show, there was this law, this disgusting law, and I thought it will not be seventy per cent, it will be one hundred per cent. Hahahahahaha.'

Jean Paul Gaultier was raised in a suburb of Paris. Both his parents were accountants. Inspiration came, he says, from his grandmother, 'a nurse and healer', who also offered extensive beauty tips to her adoring grandson. Fashion legend has it that Gaultier made his first ever conical bra for his teddy bear ('he had no sex and he had to be a woman') and that it was a grim schoolteacher who took exception to Gaultier sketching chorus girls from the Folies-Bergères ('with the fishnets and the feathers on the arse') who sealed his fate as a designer.

'She pinned the drawing to my back, you know, to shame me, and I had to go to each class and show what I had done. And, you know, I was not playing very well at football, I was not that kind of guy so I was a little rejected by the others at the school, but when I showed them they liked it. So I realised that, by sketching, people might like me. It gave me the confidence to do what I like.'

It would be all too easy to dismiss Gaultier as the lovable loon who, until recently, co-presented the high-kitsch, high-camp and, despite po-faced criticism, much-loved weekly fiasco Eurotrash alongside fellow Frenchman Antoine de Caunes. 'Antoine was so nice,' he says. 'It was like that big laugh you have when you are at school. And, you know, maybe I don't look it, but I am quite shy and Eurotrash helped me with that.'

He gave up presenting the programme, it has been said, because it was too frivolous to be taken seriously by the powers that be in French fashion – rumour has it that his exaggerated, often saucy Eurotrash persona lost Gaultier the top job at Dior.

Despite this, and the fact that he is in his mid-forties, in every piece written about him Gaultier is still described as the enfant terrible of French fashion. It is admittedly a myth he himself perpetuates, perhaps to deflect anything that might probe more deeply. He is an intensely private person who has lived alone in Paris since the death of Francis Menuge, his partner of 15 years, from Aids at the end of the Eighties. Gaultier has called Menuge his only true love.

To ignore Jean Paul Gaultier's more serious side would be to under-estimate not only his exceptional dignity and grace, but also his impact as one of the most subversive influences in 20th-century fashion. Despite commercial and critical success, however, Gaultier insists that he continues working as a designer because then 'perhaps people will like me more'. It's only fitting then that he has become one of the best-loved names in the industry.

'I am doing what I love,' says Gaultier. 'I am very passionate about it. It's what I dreamed of doing ever since I was a child. I wish for everyone to be able to do that. You know, what I do, I can do it with 'art.'

Then, and almost as if he is over-anxious not to seem too highbrow, he says it a second time, more slowly, carefully trying to pronounce that elusive 'h', though still not quite managing it.

'You know,' says Jean Paul Gaultier, 'I do eet with my 'art.'

23
YVES SAINT LAURENT

DO YOU HAVE ANY REGRETS?

NOT TO HAVE INVENTED DENIM

'Look me, but don't touch me,' says Monsieur Hector Pascual, in pigeon English and waving a white cotton-gloved finger with considerable menace. He is not, as it thankfully turns out, referring to his own diminutive if illustrious person – dressed today in immaculate silver-grey three-piece suit – but to the precious contents of one of hundreds of refrigerated clothes safes unlocked to reveal rails of the most exquisitely crafted and influential clothing designs in contemporary fashion history.

'The sleeping bee-oo-tee-fuls!' Pascual announces, lovingly lifting one piece after another to show off the workmanship, protected, for all eternity, from destruction by the elements.

First comes the 'iris' cardigan, inspired by Van Gogh's painting and made entirely by hand by the masterful house of Lesage, using, legend has it, 250,000 sequins in 22 different colours, 200,000 individually threaded pearls and 250 metres of ribbon.

Next there's the famous *Le Smoking*, the man's tuxedo reinterpreted by Saint Laurent, for the first time back in 1966, to suit a woman's needs, thereby forever relieving her of the whimsical ocean of frills and chintz that was the only possible solution to evening-wear that came before it.

In drawers beneath the rails, more garments lie between rustling sheets of pristine white tissue paper: a safari jacket rests on a trapeze-line dress, the bright colours and rich brocades of clothing inspired by the Ballets Russes on the African collection, constructed from row upon row of glittering beads.

'Look me, but don't touch me,' Pascual says again, daring any philistine to approach with bare or even unclean hands.

The setting is the Yves Saint Laurent Museum, which opened its doors to Paris and the world for the first time at the beginning of the year, to coincide with the showing of the spring/summer 2000 haute couture collection.

Hidden away in the suburbs of Paris, half an hour from the city centre, the airy space – walls of windows, polished wooden floors and huge, floor-to-ceiling, shimmering gold-leaf doors – houses no less than 5,000 outfits, 2,000 pairs of shoes, more than 10,000 pieces of jewellery and hundreds of hats.

The archive has taken some 20 years to collate, with curator Pascual working closely with M. Saint Laurent himself on the project. As well as the most important designs from the ready-to-wear and haute couture collections, stretching right back to the young Saint Laurent's time at the head of the house of Christian Dior, his sketches and costumes for film are on display.

In 1966 Saint Laurent famously dressed Catherine Deneuve for Luis Buñuel's *Belle de Jour*; 20 years later, Isabelle Adjani's clothes for Luc Besson's *Subway* also came courtesy of the designer. Yves Saint Laurent and Jean Cocteau were friends and collaborators for many years.

The museum is the only one of its kind in the world – the first given over entirely to the work of a fashion designer. But then Yves Saint Laurent, more than anyone else, is responsible for informing the way women – and indeed men – dress in the 20th century. (In this respect, only the mighty Coco Chanel comes close and, to those in the know, she was, frankly, nothing but a stylist by comparison.) The trouser suit, the black leather biker jacket, the skinny black sweater, the sheer chiffon shirt, ethnic influences from Africa to India, fashion inspired by fine art and, of course, the aforementioned tuxedo . . . all came courtesy of Saint Laurent.

Over the past 100 years, there may have been, and indeed there are still, designers of creative genius – Balenciaga, Christian Dior, Issey Miyake and Rei Kawakubo among them – but there isn't a day in the life of any modern woman reaching into her wardrobe that isn't affected by Yves Saint Laurent, and hardly a familiar item of clothing that he hasn't pioneered.

For spring/summer 2000 alone, the first season of the new millennium, every ready-to-wear label from Prada and MaxMara to Louis Vuitton and Chloe owes its inspiration to Yves Saint Laurent and the re-emergence of a style that has been variously described as everything from 'ladylike' to 'sincere chic' clothing. The *New York Times* magazine more than paid lip-service to this most auspicious of revivals at the beginning of the season, shooting the work of various major international contemporary designers in a tribute to the master and labelling the finished feature: 'It's All About Yves'.

It was like a homage to one of the great legends from the past, but if ever proof were needed of Saint Laurent's enduring resonance it came with his own haute couture collection, unveiled one week after the Saint Laurent museum opening this January.

In recognition of his huge contribution to contemporary fashion, it is Saint Laurent's privilege to close the twice-yearly haute couture collections in Paris. This season, as always, he commandeered the exuberantly ornate ballroom of the Hotel Intercontinental for the purpose. This season there was also more of a frisson than ever surrounding the proceedings.

Only the day before the show, news broke that Tom Ford – the man behind the spectacular regeneration of the Gucci label – had been installed as creative director of Yves Saint Laurent Rive Gauche men's and women's ready-to-wear, as well as the fragrance and accessory lines that prop up the label. Since last November, when Gucci acquired Sanofi – the company that previously owned the house that bears Saint Laurent's name – Ford's forthcoming appointment had been the talk of all Paris; now it had been confirmed. So this, it was assumed, was the end of an era. But what the sceptics (and perhaps Gucci themselves) had not bargained for was the ferocity of Saint Laurent's passion for haute couture.

'When the time comes, I will decide without hesitation to close down the couture house,' Pierre Bergé, for 40 years Saint Laurent's long-time business partner, former lover and closest friend, once said, at a time when Saint Laurent was physically and mentally at his lowest ebb. 'I must do that for Yves. It is a nonsense to carry on without him. Look at Chanel without Mademoiselle Chanel, and Dior without Christian Dior. It is more than nonsense. It has no integrity. It is a sham.'

True to his word, Bergé may have orchestrated the sale of Yves Saint Laurent's ready-to-wear collections, accessories, cosmetics and fragrances, but the haute couture, the jewel in the empire's crown, remained in the hands of the great man himself. And yet, as guests at Yves Saint Laurent's spring/summer 2000 haute couture collection filed in to take their tiny gilt seats and see what the master had to offer this time round, for a little while at least, all eyes were on Tom Ford, sitting front row centre alongside Domenico de Sole, Gucci's inspired chief executive. From the moment the first outfit came out onto the catwalk, however, the limelight was Saint Laurent's.

Here again was the *Le Smoking* – this time worn with frill-fronted dress shirt and bow tie. Then the safari suit in palest blue and rose, the little cocktail dresses with crisp white collars and cuffs, the sheer chiffon blouses that so outraged audiences when they were first shown. The work of the Atelier Lesage was still in evidence, too, in spellbindingly intricate beaded sweaters the colours of boiled sweets, and Romany-inspired cardigans dripping with beads.

It was a triumph to match the glory days of the Sixties and Seventies.

'Yves Saint Laurent has inspired my best fashion photos,' Helmut Newton wrote in a book celebrating the designer's 40th anniversary in fashion. 'The *Le Smoking* rue Aubriot in Paris, the man on his knees rolling down the stocking of a woman in a tailored suit at the Trocadero, a colour photo for French *Vogue* of all the mannequins in the couture salon, a series of couples in tailored suits kissing each other . . . I like the ambiguous side of his fashion for the "*grande bourgeoisie*". There are so few people with whom I feel completely in accord. And he, he is so touching, so fragile.'

It is bewildering that Yves Saint Laurent, in person, seems indeed very fragile, even demure, and this despite the fact that, now aged a grand old 63 and standing more than six feet tall, he is a quietly imposing figure, disconcertingly so.

Saint Laurent's legend casts a huge shadow over French culture. His portrait graces the last ever 5, 10 and 50 French franc pieces minted before the introduction of the Euro. On Valentine's day last year, French lovers received mail stamped with designs based on his Pop Art heart images from the 1970s. The entire refurbishment of the recently reopened Pompidou Centre was sponsored by, and is dedicated to, Yves Saint Laurent.

Yet in person he remains painfully shy. Saint Laurent may have been happy to talk in his youth; these days he is famously reclusive, rarely subjecting himself to the glare of the spotlight, and wincing at the pop of every single photographer's flashbulb. In interviews, Saint Laurent subjects journalists to excruciatingly drawn out silences, and a hesitance to offer any insights into his work that is perhaps only rivalled by Samuel Beckett's. And like Beckett, Saint Laurent is one of life's last enigmas.

This is not, it seems, through any ill will or arrogance on his part. I was once summoned to his private red-velvet-lined office upstairs at his salon in Avenue Marceau and ceremoniously thanked by Saint Laurent himself for a photo shoot I'd commissioned of his work. As he shuffled forward to meet me, with his tiny lap dog, Moujik (the subject of Andy Warhol's last portrait), held firmly under his arm, it was difficult to know which of us was more overwhelmed by the encounter, despite the fact that this was fairly obviously a momentous occasion in a young woman's fashion life.

Yves Henri Donat Mathieu Saint Laurent was born in 1936 in Oran, Algeria, to comfortably well-off parents. His father, Charles, owned a chain of cinemas. His mother, Lucienne, was a beauty who loved to entertain and doted on her son. 'I can still see my mother,' Yves Saint Laurent once wrote, 'about to leave for a ball, come to kiss me goodnight, wearing a long dress of white tulle with pear-shaped white sequins.'

Despite an idyllic home life, even at an early age Saint Laurent was overly sensitive, neurotic even, an instability that was fuelled by cruel teasing by his classmates at school. He himself maintains that this was because of his homosexuality, although there may well have been rather more that set him apart than that.

'My classmates could see I was not similar. So they made me their scapegoat. They hit me or locked me in the toilets. During the break I would take refuge in the chapel or I would arrange to stay alone in the classroom.'

If the mental breakdowns and lapses into drug and alcohol abuse that have plagued him throughout his adult life can be attributed to this bullying, the same also furnished him with a less passive side to his nature – an unswerving ambition to succeed, thereby proving his persecutors wrong. 'I told myself repeatedly: "One day you will be famous." '

On his ninth birthday, he remembers, 'I had just blown out the candles of the cake when, with a second gulp of breath, I hurled my secret wish across a table surrounded by loving relatives: "My name will be written in fiery letters on the Champs Élysées." '

Fame was not long coming to Yves Saint Laurent. At 17 he won a prize in a competition for the Wool Secretariat for a little black cocktail dress, and not long afterwards the then editor of French *Vogue* introduced him to Christian Dior, for whom he went to work at the height of his fame and the omnipotence of the New Look. Dior, by all accounts, had complete confidence in his young assistant – it was Saint Laurent, not Dior, who designed the evening dress worn in Avedon's Dovima and the Elephants, the seminal fashion image of 1955. Less than two years later, Dior died suddenly of a heart attack, leaving Saint Laurent, aged 21, presiding over France's most high-profile fashion house. He was and remains the youngest ever couturier, quickly justifying his position with a first collection of trapeze-line dresses which earned him the headline in the next day's press: 'Saint Laurent has saved France'.

In 1960 Saint Laurent was drafted into the army and promptly had a nervous breakdown. Pierre Bergé, who the designer had met just prior to being called up, visited him in hospital every day. So began the most romantic personal and creative business relationship in fashion history. By 1961 Saint Laurent was living with Bergé, who sued Dior for breach of contract when the house failed to reinstate the designer after his illness and with the proceeds set up Saint Laurent in his own business. The partners rented a two-room atelier, with a skeleton staff poached from Dior, and the rest, as they say, is history.

With Bergé at his side, providing business back-up and supporting his friend both emotionally and professionally throughout almost his entire career, Saint Laurent went on to become the world's most famous fashion designer – the epitome of Parisian style and a man whose influence has stretched far beyond his own country. It is a belief commonly expressed by designers that what they need in order to achieve immortality is a Pierre Bergé. Monsieur Bergé, touchingly, is quick to hand any such plaudits straight back to Saint Laurent.

'Of course, those designers are quite wrong when they say they need me,' he has said. 'What they need is to be a Saint Laurent.'

Saint Laurent went on to invent all the great womenswear classics and, when he opened the first of a string of Rive Gauche boutiques in 1966, put designer ready-to-wear on the map to boot. Before Saint Laurent, fashion was about haute couture – hand-stitched, exorbitantly priced outfits, designed by the great couturiers and the preserve of only the privileged few – or cheap copies cobbled together in uninspired workshops. Saint Laurent, in response to a burgeoning youth culture and a blithe, democratic spirit, changed that forever, too.

Small wonder then that the designer is constantly surrounded by a grim-faced army of PRs and a circle of close friends who have been devoted to him since his heyday – not to redirect any difficult questions but seemingly to protect his very delicate disposition from the stresses and strains of everyday life. The sense of mystique that surrounds Saint Laurent needs protecting, after all. To tarnish the legend would be a crime of fashion of unprecedented proportions.

'No more than five, or perhaps ten questions, if you please. Monsieur Saint Laurent, 'e is very delicate, you see,' I am instructed, having agreed to interview the designer by fax rather than talk to him in person a second time.

Miraculously, within 48 hours, he responded.

SF: Of all the things you have ever designed, which is the one thing you most cherish?
YSL: The *Le Smoking* because it gave freedom to the woman. It also gave the woman the confidence to feel beautiful.
SF: What is the most exciting thing in fashion today?
YSL: No more rules, the freedom of dressing. The beauty of mixing vintage clothes with a pair of jeans that I love.
SF: Is haute couture the most precious side of your work?
YSL: Yes, it is. I am very happy to design haute couture. It's a love story between couture and me.
SF: What has been the most exciting time of your life?
YSL: My first show in 1962, rue Spontini, and when I was honoured to be asked by Diana Vreeland to set up an exhibition of my work at the Metropolitan in New York in 1983.
SF: What makes you most happy?
YSL: To come every day to 5 Avenue Marceau, all the people there are like my children. Seeing Cubism paintings at the Beaubourg makes me very happy and also old films.
SF: Do you have any regrets?
YSL: Not to have invented denim.
SF: What is it that most inspires you?
YSL: The fashion of the street.